Magazine Production

Magazine Production presents a guide to the practical processes of taking a magazine from initial idea to final product. This second edition provides important revisions on these production processes by examining the technological and business advancements which have reshaped the magazine industry in the last decade. Brand new chapters document the rise of digital media and identify its impact on magazine creation. They also include new guidance on designing online, tablet and mobile editions, as well as for print.

Magazine Production explains the business of magazines in the UK, Europe and North America, and the roles of marketing, publishing and advertising in establishing a successful title. This edition also addresses the move by publishers towards e-commerce, multimedia content and events to promote their brands and sell products. With information on professional bodies such as the Professional Publishers Association, an expert overview of magazine markets and a breakdown of roles within editorial and design departments, this book offers readers practical steps to achieving success in magazine publishing today.

Magazine Production includes:

- an introduction to the history, markets and audiences of magazines
- explanations of the roles of publishers and advertising teams as part of the business of magazines
- a comparison between print and new systems of digital circulation, with particular focus on mobile platforms;
- guidance on setting up editorial teams, and best practice for producing feature, news and review copy
- information on designing and laying out a title for print or digital distribution
- legal and ethical issues affecting magazine editors and publishers
- a consideration of the future of magazines.

Jason Whittaker is Head of the School of English and Journalism at the University of Lincoln, UK, with a special responsibility for magazine production and contextual studies. He has over 15 years' experience as a journalist, and ten years as an editor with a special interest in IT and B2B titles. He is the author of numerous academic books and articles including *Producing for Web 2.0* (2009).

Media Skills

EDITED BY RICHARD KEEBLE, LINCOLN UNIVERSITY

The *Media Skills* series provides a concise and thorough introduction to a rapidly changing media landscape. Each book is written by media and journalism lecturers or experienced professionals and is a key resource for a particular industry. Offering helpful advice and information and using practical examples from print, broadcast and digital media, as well as discussing ethical and regulatory issues, *Media Skills* books are essential guides for students and media professionals.

Designing for Newspapers and Magazines
2nd edition
Chris Frost

English for Journalists
Twentieth Anniversary Edition
Wynford Hicks

Ethics for Journalists
2nd edition
Richard Keeble

Feature Writing for Journalists
Sharon Wheeler

Freelancing for Television and Radio
Leslie Mitchell

Interviewing for Journalists
2nd edition
Sally Adams, with Wynford Hicks

Interviewing for Radio
2nd edition
Jim Beaman

Magazine Production
2nd edition
Jason Whittaker

Programme Making for Radio
Jim Beaman

Production Management for Television
Leslie Mitchell

Researching for the Media
2nd edition
Adèle Emm

Reporting for Journalists
2nd edition
Chris Frost

Subediting and Production for Journalists
2nd edition
Tim Holmes

Writing for Broadcast Journalists
2nd edition
Rick Thompson

Writing for Journalists
3rd edition
Wynford Hicks with Sally Adams, Harriett Gilbert, Tim Holmes and Jane Bentley

Magazine Production

SECOND EDITION

Jason Whittaker

Routledge
Taylor & Francis Group

LONDON AND NEW YORK

Second edition published 2017
by Routledge
2 Park Square, Milton Park, Abingdon, Oxon OX14 4RN

and by Routledge
711 Third Avenue, New York, NY 10017

Routledge is an imprint of the Taylor & Francis Group, an informa business

First edition published by Routledge 2008

British Library Cataloguing in Publication Data
A catalogue record for this book is available from the British Library

Library of Congress Cataloging in Publication Data
Names: Whittaker, Jason, 1969– author.
Title: Magazine production / Jason Whittaker.
Description: 2nd edition. | London; New York: Routledge, 2016. |
Series: Media skills | Includes bibliographical references and index.
Identifiers: LCCN 2016020495 | ISBN 9781138122147 (hardback : alk. paper) |
ISBN 9781138122154 (pbk. : alk. paper) | ISBN 9781315650616 (ebook)
Subjects: LCSH: Periodicals—Publishing—Handbooks, manuals, etc. | Magazine
design—Handbooks, manuals, etc.
Classification: LCC Z286.P4 W48 2016 | DDC 070.5/72—dc23
LC record available at https://lccn.loc.gov/2016020495

ISBN: 978-1-138-12214-7 (hbk)
ISBN: 978-1-138-12215-4 (pbk)
ISBN: 978-1-315-65061-6 (ebk)

Typeset in Goudy
by Keystroke, Neville Lodge, Tettenhall, Wolverhampton

To Sam, for all her patience

Contents

Illustrations

Figures

Tables

Introduction

Magazines fill our daily lives. Often we encounter them casually – as filler when we are waiting for an appointment, or something to read while travelling by train. At other times, they are the focus for interests, hobbies and our professional life, something that we subscribe to or actively seek out because they are the best source of information on a particular subject.

Since the publication of the first edition of this book, magazine production has undergone some profound changes. In the first decade of the twenty-first century, plenty of magazine publishers were starting to launch web sites, but most were struggling to find a way to make money from those sites and nearly all the attention – certainly for the most important titles – remained firmly fixed on print. Two particular elements have changed this approach to digital: first of all, social media emerged in that decade as perhaps the most important means of connecting people ever seen and, like all media companies, magazine publishers had to start taking a digital strategy seriously.

More dramatically for the future of print titles, when Apple launched the first iPhone in 2007 the world of mobile began to have an impact on magazines just as the web more generally had affected newspapers during the previous decade. While it took a little while for these changes to be felt, when Apple followed the iPhone with the iPad in 2010 it became clear that more and more readers preferred consuming media on a screen rather than through the printed pages of a magazine.

Alongside these extremely important changes in the digital sphere, magazines have started to realise that they must operate across a broad range of categories, with titles now frequently producing audio and video materials for readers alongside the text and images that they have worked with for more than a century. All of it, of course, must be made available through a panoply of social media, and for many titles their main interactions with consumers will not be within the confines of a bound periodical. For that reason, magazines increasingly refer to themselves as brands – a series of expert opinions and world views that can be encountered in a huge variety of formats.

Brands fall into two broad categories: those aimed at the consumer and those which are designed for professionals or people working in an industry or business. In addition, there are other periodicals produced for an academic or highly specialised market, such as science and medicine, or the arts and humanities. In addition, many of the most specialised titles today are increasingly produced in digital only editions, whether for the web or mobile. These tend to have very restricted circulations and very little, if any, advertising. As such, they are not covered in the following chapters which focus, instead, on commercial titles.

This book concentrates on magazine production, the skills needed to create a magazine in terms of editorial, and design for print and digital formats. However, it also aims to provide the reader with a background to some elements of magazine publishing, and outline the main players in the UK and worldwide market.

Different chapters deal with the role of the publisher and the importance of advertising, as well as various elements of magazine business such as distribution, circulation and marketing. Although these would not necessarily be immediately important for students working on a magazine for college or university, anyone who hopes to break into the magazine industry should have a solid understanding of the business side of publishing. What is more, editors need to deal with publishers, advertising sales teams, marketing managers, circulation directors and digital strategists on a regular basis, and the demands of these various departments all feed into the production of a commercial title.

An important aim of this book, then, is to introduce the reader to key terminology, contexts and practices in the magazine industry, explaining the differences between consumer and business-to-business (B2B) sectors, the financial requirements and business of publishing. The main part of the book also works through the abilities and skills that are required to take a magazine from initial concept to finished product.

Chapter 1 provides an overview of the magazine industry, tracing its history and looking in some detail at the types of publications on offer and the main publishers. There is also an introduction to the role of the Professional Publishers Association, the main industry body for magazines.

Chapter 2 concentrates on the business of publishing, looking in particular at the role of the publisher and how he or she relates to other departments on a typical commercial magazine. Although the main focus of this book is magazine production, some understanding of how other departments, such as advertising, work will be useful for those seeking a job in magazines.

Chapter 3 looks at the ways in which magazine production has been transformed in the past decade, with the rise of mobile devices in particular. Even for those titles which still operate in a print-only format, the transformation in consumers' reading habits means that all brands now must consider a digital strategy as part of their operations.

The next three chapters deal with the production process proper, beginning with editorial and copy in Chapter 4. After discussing the role of the editor, and how a typical magazine editorial department is structured, this chapter goes on to discuss the type of planning cycles that need to be put in place to make a title successful. It also considers the main types of article that appear in publications – news, features and reviews – with a brief account of the role of commissioning editors.

A good magazine does not simply consist of text, however, so Chapter 5 looks at the role of the art editor and the importance of good design in creating compelling publications for print. This chapter concentrates on typography, colour and graphics (photography and illustration), all of which are brought together in a final layout and prepared for the printers.

Chapter 6 considers some of the practicalities of setting up your brand for the digital environment. As well as taking into account social media, computers and mobile devices offer a particularly rich experience for multimedia, and this chapter will offer guidance for building video production into your workflow as well as what to look for when producing for tablets or smartphones.

In Chapter 7 readers are given a concise overview of the main legal and ethical challenges that face magazine editors and journalists, in particular libel and copyright. Here readers will also find information about some of the professional bodies that affect journalism in the UK, such as the National Union of Journalists (NUJ) and the Independent Press Standards Organisation (IPSO).

Finally, while this book takes into account the changes of the past decade that have affected magazine brands most dramatically, it is also clear that there are still many more changes to come, some of which will be considered as part of the future of the magazine industry.

1
Magazines and their markets

Magazines in the digital age

The history of magazines is nearly as old as that of newspapers, periodicals having first begun to circulate in Europe in the seventeenth century and becoming more widely available during the eighteenth. For the past three hundred years, they have been the most diverse form of print media in terms of content, markets and physical formats, and today are transforming into a variety of publications designed for digital consumption, especially via tablets and smartphones.

It is with regard to markets and content that the real range of magazines can be seen. From weekly news-digest titles and monthly general men's and women's magazines, to specialist titles for particular consumer and professional interests, before the rise of the internet no other medium focused on specific niche markets to the same degree.

Magazines are often referred to as periodicals, and it is the regular nature of their appearance – not daily like most national and many regional newspapers, but weekly, monthly or at other set times during the year – that has often defined their status although, as with many other formats, the rise of digital distribution is having an effect on rolling news via the web in particular. As the majority of titles tend to be much more specific than newsprint, the calendar of events for such things as fashion shows, new car launches or the holiday seasons punctuate the ebb and flow of information that we have come to expect from the glossies.

Types of magazine

To stretch the definition of magazines to some degree, some would probably also include newsletters in this category (which have increasingly moved into email inboxes over the past decade). Since the turn of the century, many magazines have gone online, first to the web and then in digital editions designed to be read on a tablet or phone. In many cases, such digital editions are intended as supplements to a printed version, but several ezines – such as *Salon* (salon.com) or *Rue* (ruemag.com) – have only ever existed online. Similarly, some titles – such as *PC World* (pcworld.com) and *Jet* (jetmag.com) – ceased print publication and became entirely digital. Not that print is by any means dead. When *Newsweek* announced that it was going digital only in 2013, its acquisition by a new owner, International Business Times, as well as a rise in profitability, saw a print relaunch in 2014.

Of course, what is very different to digital publications is the ability to provide multimedia that brings together audio and video, part of the process of convergence that is affecting media around the world – and with which, it must be noted, some traditional publishers are struggling to come to terms as they see their audiences shift online.

In the past five years, perhaps the most dramatic change for such audiences has been the rise of tablets as an increasingly popular way to consume a whole range of media. Tablet computers were first developed in the 1990s, but these bulky and expensive devices did not become popular until the launch of Apple's iPad in 2010. With a larger screen than smartphones, such devices are better suited to sophisticated layouts that have often been the hallmark of magazines, with almost 220 million tablets having been sold in 2013. Sales have actually declined a little since that high point mainly because, in contrast to phones, consumers tend not to upgrade their devices as often, but with many families tending to own more than one tablet per household they have become the standard means for enjoying many different types of entertainment.

Apple itself attempted to exploit this fact when it launched Newsstand (often referred to as an app, including by Apple itself, but actually a special folder in the operating system iOS 7) in 2011 as a home for newspapers and magazines on the iPad. With the release of iOS 9 in 2015 this was replaced by News, which brings together discrete articles from across the web rather than fully downloadable magazines, a factor that indicates the changing face of the periodical market today. Alternatives to Newsstand include Zinio (launched in 2001), which distributes more than 5,000 magazines, and Texture (previously First Issue), often described as a Netflix for magazines.

While apps such as Zinio and Texture offer complete magazines to readers (sometimes little more than PDF versions of the print edition), a more radical change is likely to be the shift towards social media aggregators such as Flipboard or Pulse. These draw articles from a range of online sources, often reformatting web pages in a way that is easier to read on a tablet or phone. While they may offer sections that are discrete to particular publications, more frequently the magazines on offer are curated by staff working for the app companies themselves or even created by consumers who may then share their personalised collections.

The popularity of magazines

Despite the growth of the World Wide Web, new media and technologies have not diminished the popularity of magazines. Traditionally, magazines have tended to be divided into two types: consumer and specialised business titles, the latter once referred to as trade magazines but more often now as business-to-business, or B2B. Consumer magazines will carry a great deal of advertising and be available in a wide number of outlets, while B2B titles are usually only available to a restricted number of readers – something that will be considered in much more detail in Chapter 3.

According to British Rates and Data (BRAD), the total number of magazines published in the UK in 2014 was 7,053 (a decline from more than 8,500 brands in 2006), of which 2,958 were consumer magazines and 4,095 aimed at the B2B sector. In the USA, about 1,000 companies published magazines with a combined annual subscription and sales revenue of more than $14 billion in 2013 and advertising revenues of another $15 billion. Despite the decline of print circulations in the past decade, Time Warner alone sold more than 32 million magazines in 2013.

In the UK, the Advertising Association observes that advertising revenues for magazines increased from £499 million in 1994 to £993 million in 2015, although that also includes a fall from more than £1.5 billion in 2007. Much of this recent decline is due to internet advertising, which grew literally from nothing to be worth nearly £8 billion during the same period (and which is still growing rapidly).

The National Readership Survey (NRS) reported in 2015 that 94 per cent of adults read a newspaper or magazine in print or digital format, and though there has been a very slight decline in magazine readership since 2007 (from 75 per cent to 73 per cent) they remain popular. The biggest change has been in the 15+ age range: whereas 80 per cent read a print magazine in 2007, that has now declined to 63 per cent, although 38 per cent consume such brands via their mobile device. Ever since they became a fixture of modern life at the end of the nineteenth century, part of the modern mass media that shaped our perceptions of the past 120 years, we have used magazines to develop our tastes, pursue our gossip, improve our professional life and serve as a window on the world about us.

The beginnings of magazines

Magazines in Western Europe first began to appear in substantial numbers during the early eighteenth century, although their format was closer to that of news sheets, pamphlets and books than what we would recognise as magazines today. The original meaning of the word as a store for a variety of goods indicates the most significant difference between early magazines and the first newspapers that were published in Britain during the seventeenth century.

Rather than being restricted to news, magazines quickly established themselves as a forum for gentlemen editors and writers to espouse their opinions on a whole range of subjects, such as fashion and literary taste as well as politics and religion.

Although magazines had been published on the Continent in the seventeenth century, the first English magazine is typically taken to be Daniel Defoe's *The Review* (1704–13), which began the year after Defoe had been imprisoned for criticising the Church of England. The purpose of *The Review*, issued as four pages of densely printed text with few illustrations, was to offer comment and satire on the state of the nation, but the most famous of these early journals were *The Tatler* (1709) and *The Spectator* (1711–14), which were edited respectively by Joseph Addison and Richard Steele and included articles by many famous literary contributors such as Alexander Pope and Jonathan Swift.

Addison and Steele pioneered the short, informal essay, the elegant precursor of the feature article, establishing a new role for the modern journalist in the first issue of *The Spectator*:

> I have observed, that a Reader seldom peruses a Book with Pleasure 'till he knows whether the Writer of it be a black or a fair Man, of a mild or cholerick Disposition, Married or a Batchelor, with other Particulars of the like nature, that conduce very much to the right Understanding of an Author ... I have passed my latter Years in this City, where I am frequently seen in most publick Places, tho' there are not above half a dozen of my select Friends that know me. There is no place of Resort wherein I do not often make my appearance; sometimes I am seen thrusting my Head into a Round of Politicians at 'Will's' and listning with great Attention to the Narratives that are made in those little Circular Audiences. Sometimes I smoak a Pipe at 'Child's' and, while I seem attentive to nothing but the Post-Man, over-hear the Conversation of every Table in the Room ... Thus I live in the World, rather as a Spectator of Mankind, than as one of the Species; by which means I have made my self a Speculative Statesman, Soldier, Merchant, and Artizan, without ever medling with any Practical Part in Life ... In short, I have acted in all the parts of my Life as a Looker-on, which is the Character I intend to preserve in this Paper.
> No. 1, 1 March 1711

The Gentleman's *Magazine:*

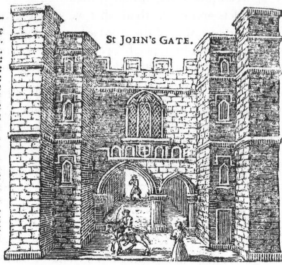

St John's Gate.

Lond Gazette
Londō Jour.
Fog's Journ.
Applebee's ::
Head's :: : :
Craftsman ::
D. Spectator
Grubstreet J
W.ly Register
Free = Briton
Hpp = Doctor
Daily Court.
Daily = Post
Dai. = ournal
Da. Post-boy
D. Advertiser
Evening Post
St James's Eb.
Whitehall En.
Lōdon Ebēfg
=lving = Post
Weekly Mif-
cellany.

Pozk 2 News
Dublin 6 :::
Edinburgh 2
Bristol :: : :
Norwich 2 ::
Exeter 2 :
Worcester :
Northampton
Gloucester : :
Stamford : :
Nottingham
Burp Journ
Chester ditto
Derby ditto
Ipswich dit.
Reading dit.
Leeds Merc.
Newcastle C.
Canterbury
Manchester
Boston ::: ¶
Jamaica, &c
Barbados :

Or, MONTHLY INTELLIGENCER.

For JANUARY, 1731.

CONTAINING,

/moze in Quantity, and greater Variety, than any Book of the Kind and Price./

I. A VIEW of the WEEKLY ESSAYS, *viz.* Of Queen *Elizabeth* ; Ministers ; Treaties ; Liberty of the Press ; Riot Act ; Armies ; Traytors ; Patriots ; Reason ; Criticism ; Versifying ; Ridicule ; Humours ; Love ; Prostitutes ; Musick ; Pawn-brokers ; Surgery ; Law.

II. POETRY. The Ode for the New Year, by *Colly Cibber*, Esq; Remarks upon it ; Imitations of it, by way of *Burlesque* ; Verses on the same Subject ; ingenious Epitaphs and Epigrams.

III. DOMESTICK OCCURRENCES ; *viz.* Births, Deaths, Marriages, Preferments,

Casualties, Burials and Christenings in *London.*

IV. Melancholy Effects of Credulity in *Witchcraft.*

V. Prices of Goods, Grain, Stocks, and a List of Bankrupts.

VI. A correct List of the Sheriffs for the current Year.

VII. Remarkable Advertisements.

VIII. FOREIGN Affairs, with an Introduction to this Year's History.

IX. REGISTER of Books.

X. Observations on Gardening.

XI. Table of CONTENTS.

By *SYLVANUS URBAN*, Gent.

The FIFTH EDITION.

LONDON: Printed for the AUTHOR, and sold at St *John's Gate :* By F. *Jefferies,* in *Ludgate-street* ; all other Booksellers ; and by the Persons who serve Gentlemen with the News-papers : *Of whom may be had* Compleat Sets, *or any* single Number.

A few are printed on ROYAL PAPER, *large Margin,* for the CURIOUS.

Figure 1.1 *The Gentleman's Magazine*, 1731

The figure of the objective spectator – committed to no party and capable of spotting the errors of any mere practitioner – was soon to become an established component of eighteenth-century literary and political journalism. The growth of a bourgeois public sphere in London, centred on the new wealth of a capitalist empire, brought with it new opportunities and new anxieties.

Under a feudal system, rank and custom had been clearly defined by birth and ownership of land, but in this new order the role of gentleman was increasingly demarcated (and, for many, increasingly defiled) by wealth alone. For the *nouveaux riches*, lacking centuries of tradition on how to behave, literary publications such as *The Spectator* provided necessary instruction on what to do in public.

One clear example of the significance of this new genre was *The Gentleman's Magazine*. Founded in 1731 by Edward Cave, it was one of the most successful magazines ever issued, not ceasing publication until 1907. Cave's original intention had been to provide a monthly digest of news and commentary, and the early issues of his title were a rich miscellany of information that no gentleman could afford to miss, including essays, poetry, extracts from new works and informative articles on religion and politics as well as endless lists on all topics from county sheriffs to bankrupts. Samuel Johnson was one of its more famous contributors, and Cave's canny business sense led to *The Gentleman's Magazine* being distributed throughout the English-speaking world.

For nearly two centuries after their initial appearance, magazines were largely the preserve of the upper classes. Relatively expensive to produce (certainly compared with later publications), late eighteenth- and early nineteenth-century titles such as *Blackwoods* and the *Edinburgh Review* tended to concentrate on literature and serious comment, with a rather austere format that changed little before the final decades of the nineteenth century.

Technological innovation and the rise of mass media

The transformation of magazines into a mass commodity relied on two inter-related developments, innovations in technology and the rise of a mass media, both of which, in turn, depended on wider economic and social changes in Europe and North America.

Technological developments involved improvements in presswork, the process of transferring impressions to paper, and composition, creating readable type. The invention of lithography by Alois Senefelder in the late 1790s, and its subsequent enhancements in the following years, enabled the reproduction of text and image more cheaply than the laborious engraving techniques that had been used until that time.

By applying a waxy crayon to limestone, Senefelder could etch the plate surface with acid to leave a relief which was resistant to water: when the plate was dampened, ink could easily be applied and would not hold on the wet parts of the stone. Modern lithography uses photography to transfer an image to a metal plate or, with computer-to-plate (CTP) technology, the image is drawn by laser: in addition, the refinement of offset lithography, whereby the image from the plate is transferred to a rubber blanket before printing it onto paper, meant that images and text could be printed the correct way round.

While this process revolutionised presswork, composition was transformed radically by the invention of the Linotype machine by Ottmar Mergenthaler in 1886. Prior to this, individual letters of text were assembled by hand, but Mergenthaler's machine allowed a typesetter to retrieve a set of moulds, or matrices, of imprinted letters into which molten lead was poured to create a line of text. Because hand composition had been so time consuming, newspapers were restricted to a few pages; this was less of an issue with magazines, which did not need to be produced daily, but all forms of journalism benefited from the invention of hot-metal typesetting. Although eventually replaced by photographic lithography, the Linotype provided a huge advance in magazine production.

Printing presses themselves also underwent significant developments: the steam press, devised in 1812, enabled more than 1,000 pages to be printed per hour, while the rotary printing press (1833) increased this to a million copies of a page in a single day.

Technological innovations themselves, however, brought about by the improved manufacturing processes of industrialised societies, were not enough to create a mass media. The conditions that led to mass audiences included increased literacy rates (enabled in England, for example, by government-financed public education in 1870) and the increase in spare capital among the working classes that meant they could spend more on consumer commodities. By the final decade of the nineteenth century, entrepreneurial publishers were realising that they could take advantage of these new conditions.

In the USA in 1893, Samuel McClure released his literary and political *McClure's Magazine* at the low price of 15 cents, a title that published writers such as Arthur Conan Doyle and Rudyard Kipling, and which specialised in investigative journalism known as muckraking to its detractors (a phenomenon linked to the so-called sensationalist 'yellow journalism' that emerged during the circulation battles between Joseph Pulitzer and William Randolph Hearst in the late 1890s). Rival Frank Munsey cut the price of *Munsey's Magazine* to 10 cents, with both publishers seeking to attain higher profits through advertising rather than cover price.

Figure 1.2 Der Dada, 1920

The contrast between this new breed of journalism and the genteel literary magazines became more pronounced at the turn of the century. As well as *Munsey's Magazine*, Frank Munsey had launched a title aimed at children called *Argosy*; costing 5 cents and comprising eight pages, it was not initially a success, but, relaunched as a title for adults at the end of the decade, it instituted the rise of the pulp magazines (so called because they were made from low-grade paper, in contrast to the 'slicks' aimed at more affluent readers).

From the 1920s to the 1950s, these pulp titles were published in increasing numbers and introduced what was, in some respects, a golden age of magazine publishing. While content was often of a quality that did not even match the paper it was printed on, the pulps were often great innovators in genre publishing, especially detective, horror and science fiction, providing a market for new writers in titles such as *Amazing Stories*, *Black Mask* and *Weird Tales*. The format was eventually to face decline from rising costs and competition from comics, television and cheap paperback novels.

The design revolution

Technological innovations such as lithography meant that by 1900 magazines looked very different to the journals of a hundred years previously. Illustrations were now commonplace and the physical format of the magazine was similar to that of modern publications, with two further important developments being the invention of photography and the contribution of modernism to the field of design.

By the final decade of the nineteenth century, photography had been in existence for nearly half a century, but the ability to mass produce photographs was extremely limited (for example, publishers would hire engravers to copy a photograph so that it could be transferred to print). The growing number of magazines in the early twentieth century fuelled the demand for more photographic illustrations, which in turn could be reproduced more easily by refinements to lithographic printing, while the development of lighter camera equipment such as the German-manufactured Ermanox and Leica compact cameras in the 1920s contributed to the growth of photojournalism.

Photography had been used to document important events since the American Civil War, but during the 1920s photo magazines increased in number. Publications such as the *Müncher Illustrierte Presse* and *Berliner Illustrierte Zeitung* began to publish a new style of spontaneous image, defined by Henri Cartier-Bresson as the 'decisive moment', which became enormously popular with the reading public. It was during the 1930s, however, with titles including *Life*

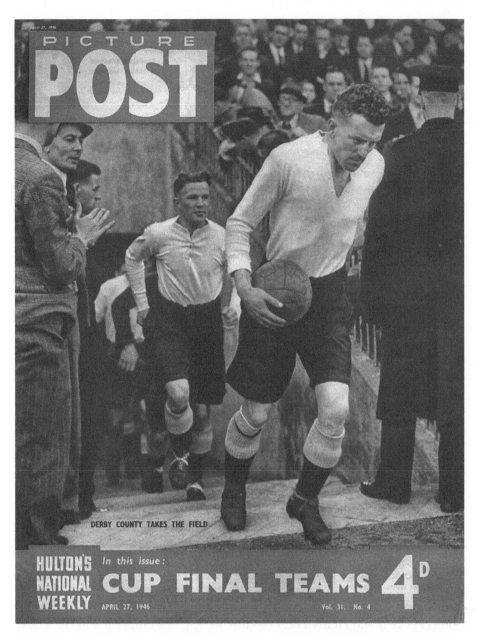

Figure 1.3 Picture Post, 1946. Image courtesy of Picture Post/Getty Images.

(1936) in the USA and *Picture Post* (1938) in the UK, that photography became a staple of magazine production.

Alongside the important contribution of photography and photojournalism, the format of magazine publishing was being revolutionised by the art of the avant-garde. While the new artistic forms of cubism, Dadaism, futurism and surrealism appeared very far from the mass consumerism of the muckraking or yellow press, many modern artists were fascinated by contemporary technology and culture. Initially, their experiments were confined to small-scale manifestos and journals, but the typographic and sophisticated graphic design pursued by publications such as *Der Dada, 391* and *Minotaure* were taken up by advertisers and commercial magazine publishers in the inter-war period.

At the time of their publication, such periodicals operated outside the mainstream of magazine publishing and the dominant public sphere that most companies were interested in. The radical press had been a common feature of the newspaper press during the nineteenth century before gradually been squeezed out by the demands of advertising in particular, but the relative ease with which magazines could be produced meant that an alternative press – of which such modernist titles were a part – continued to flourish throughout the twentieth century. Just as early twentieth-century artists sought to connect to a discriminating audience, so a range of alternative titles would seek to cater to readers connected by politics, taste and sexuality.

For the mainstream, however, advertising was incredibly important to fuelling growth. Ad agencies, which were first established during the 1890s, very quickly saw the appeal of new graphic formats, employing slogans, photography and bold imagery to grab the attention of consumers. As with other mass-media formats (particularly poster art during the early twentieth century), advertising became extremely important to magazine publishers as a means to sell titles below cost. Successful magazine designers were often those who had also worked for advertisers, and as full-page display advertising became the norm so editorial pages had to be more innovative to compete for the reader's attention.

It was during the inter-war period that one of the most important media companies of the twentieth century was created. *Time* was launched in 1923 by Briton Hadden and Henry Luce, the first weekly news magazine in the USA, and the pair established a publishing empire that would include *Fortune* (1930), *Life* (1936), *Sports Illustrated* (1954) and *People* (1974).

By the time of Luce's death in 1967, TimeInc. was worth $109 million and, following the merger with Warner Communications in 1990, became part of the world's largest media and entertainment company. This title was only recently surpassed by Google – although the new media company has a much lower turnover. Despite current downsizing of its portfolio of 150 titles, Time Warner is still the largest magazine publishing company in the USA, with a market value of $78 billion on sales of $42 billion in 2005.

The rise of the glossies

In the 1920s, pulp magazines were sometimes compared to the 'slicks', particularly fashion magazines such as *Vogue* that were printed on higher-quality paper with professional photography and full colour on most, if not all, pages. It was not until the 1950s, however, that the full benefits of earlier innovations in design combined with a consumer boom after a period of post-war austerity to produce the contemporary glossy in all its glory.

Alongside mainstream consumer publications, the post-war period also saw a surge of interest in the alternative press, particularly from the 1960s onwards. While these did not fit into the more general trend of magazines as glossies, mainly because of the higher production costs associated with such publications, they were an incredibly important means of communicating ideas that were ignored in the dominant public sphere. During the twentieth century, the underground press served an incredibly important function in countries such as Czechoslovakia, producing a stream of *samizdat* titles that offered counter-views to the communist authorities, but also in the West magazines and papers such as *International Times* and *Oz* were regularly promoting ideas and lifestyles associated with the left-wing counter-culture.

In the 1930s, the first steps to recuperate the men's magazine market were taken by the publication of *Men Only* (1935) in the UK and *Esquire* (1933) in the USA. As well as including that popular staple, the pin-up (only later to develop into more fully fledged pornography), these titles included articles, features and fashion pages designed for what publishers and advertisers saw as a sophisticated and affluent market.

By the middle of the century, men's magazines were seen as largely synonymous with pornography (for which *Playboy*, launched in 1953, bore some responsibility, although its publisher, Hugh Hefner, saw it as an extension of *Esquire* for which he had previously worked). Colour weekend supplements, such as those for the *Sunday Times*, attracted the advertising base that had previously read more general publications, and the entire market languished until the 1980s when titles such as *GQ* and *Arena* were imported to the UK from the USA.

However, the real shake-up of the market was seen in 1994, with the launch of *Loaded*: its irreverent attitude under the editorial lead of James Brown saw sales of over a quarter of a million by 1996, and it was quickly followed by a raft of titles such as *FHM* (bought by Emap from Tayvale) and *Maxim*. The market for men's magazines, however, proved short-lived in the internet age. *FHM*, after a high point of more than 600,000 sales early in the twenty-first century closed in 2015 and *Loaded* itself ceased as a print magazine in the March of that year before returning (sans half-clothed women) as a digital-only title in November 2015.

During the final decades of the twentieth century, the glossy look that had originally been pioneered by *Vogue*, *Esquire* and *Playboy* had now extended even into the trade and B2B sectors. In addition, the 1980s saw further technological developments which, in their own way, were as significant as the inventions of lithographic printing and photography.

The introduction of computers and desktop publishing saw radical changes to the ways that magazines were produced, with smaller teams capable of taking a title from initial conception to final print much more quickly and – once the technology had become widespread – more cheaply than ever before. By the early 1990s, it was predicted that magazine publishing would be opened up to a more democratic process; in one respect, while it did become more profitable to engage in more and more niche publishing (particularly in the business market, which exploded from this period onwards), in reality the difficulties and costs of actually printing and distributing a magazine, as opposed simply to preparing copy and layouts, saw the consolidation of publishing houses continue apace into the twenty-first century.

Digital developments and mobile

The invention of the web in the 1990s began to affect magazine publishing as it did every other platform, providing the opportunity for a worldwide distribution system that was extremely difficult to implement prior to that period.

Two early innovations in terms of digital magazine publishing were Pathfinder and HotWired, both launched in 1994 and representing very different approaches to the new medium. Pathfinder, owned by Time Warner, was a portal to some 80 content providers, mostly magazines produced by the company such as *Time*, *People* and *Fortune*. While this allowed the company to distribute an almost unprecedented amount of content (much of it, for a short period of time, freely available to users), this was largely 'shovelware' – static PDFs or images of printed pages uploaded to the web. The site was not especially popular with either users or producers, and closed in 1999 having cost Time Warner an estimated $100–120 million.

Figure 1.4 Vogue, 1950. Abstract close-up of model Jean Pratchett's eye with heavy eyeliner make-up. Image courtesy of Erwin Blumenfeld/ Vogue; © Condé Nast.

By contrast, HotWired took a very different approach to the web as the digital companion to *Wired* magazine. *Wired* was founded in 1993 to provide commentary and analysis on the digital age, using journalistic and design styles commonly associated with glossy lifestyle magazines rather than the more staid, traditional computer press. The founders of *Wired* saw the web as an essential component of their business model and the site was more than a repository for the print title's content. Instead, HotWired produced original news and features, taking advantage of rolling publishing deadlines to keep readers up to date. Although HotWired itself closed in 1999, it spun off a number of side projects and sites before becoming Wired News.

The growth of the internet was also extremely important in promoting the availability of alternative magazines. In addition to taking advantage of the simplicity of distribution offered by the web, activist publications in particular allow readers to engage with titles that often take a very different approach to publication in contrast to mainstream brands, being run along co-operative lines by the editorial team rather than in a conventional, hierarchically organised structure. Many of these had already developed alternative distribution channels in the age of print (via charities, trade unions, political parties or through radical bookshops), but the extension of the internet increased their reach greatly, as in the example of *Counterpunch* (counterpunch.org), an internet magazine that is also available to subscribers as a high-quality PDF.

During the first decade of the twenty-first century, for many magazines the web had much less of an impact than on newspapers, with print sales and advertising largely holding up apart from a few exceptions, most notably the technology sector, where online publishing quickly cannibalised print. Readers generally seemed to prefer the format and feel of print in contrast to reading layouts on a screen. The real change came with the widespread adoption of tablets from 2010.

Prior to Apple's iPad, tablet computers had been bulky devices with poor battery life and operating systems that largely betrayed their dependence on a mouse and keyboard. With the launch of the iPhone in 2007, Apple had demonstrated the real virtues of an operating system that relied solely on touch, and with further innovations such as a high-resolution ('retina') display the new generation of tablets was quickly adopted by users – Apple sold a million iPads within a month – as a means to consume a range of media, including web sites, films, photographs, books and magazines.

With regard to magazines, despite the quick adaptation by companies such as Zinio of their products as apps for the new device, tablets initially did very little to challenge the popularity of print media. By the second decade of the twenty-first century, however, many publishers were starting to suffer as the web was changing consumer habits, combined with the general economic malaise caused by the crash of 2008 which meant there was less money to spend on advertising.

Magazine publishers began to create their own apps for the iPad (and then Android devices), but Apple's launch of Newsstand in 2011 was hailed by the company as the salvation of magazines and newspapers, bringing together content in one convenient location. Unfortunately, neither Newsstand nor the alternatives such as Zinio addressed the fundamental change in reading habits that were taking place with magazines just as habits were changing in just about every medium, such as news, television and music. As consumers were less willing to pay for a complete album when they really only wanted to listen to one track, so it was clear that fewer readers wanted to purchase a subscription to a magazine when all they desired was one or two articles from that publication.

It is certainly true that the business models developed during the nineteenth century and perfected in the twentieth have struggled to adapt in the twenty-first, but the idea of a store house for a miscellany of entertaining and inform-ative articles that go beyond the news remains as important as ever. Publications such as *Wired* have, unsurprisingly, jumped at the opportunities provided by the slick, easy-to-use interfaces offered by iOS and Android, while stalwarts such as *The Atlantic* (first published in 1857) are as beautiful in a tablet app as they are in print. Where the biggest revolution is taking place, however, is via social

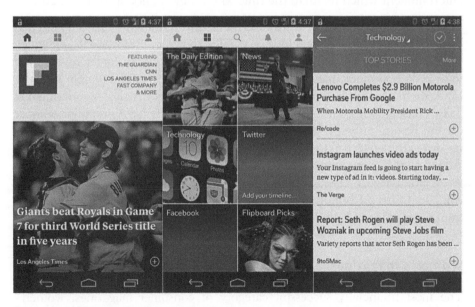

Figure 1.5 The Flipboard newsreader app

media aggregators such as Flipboard and LinkedIn Pulse, which bring together content from a variety of online sources. Flipboard advertises itself as 'Your personal magazine', moving away from the traditional notion of issues created centrally by publishers to eclectic collections curated by individuals.

Markets and audiences

The development of magazines into a format that is instantly recognisable more or less anywhere in the world has been accompanied by a much greater segmentation of the magazine market. Unlike just about any other medium until the rise of the internet and digital television, magazines are usually aimed at very specific, niche audiences, with readerships often numbering in the low thousands or tens of thousands.

Consumer magazines

In terms of quantities of copies sold, consumer magazines dominate the news-stands. There are many more specialist trade and B2B titles, but the bestselling magazines are general men's and women's titles, as well as television guides, and leisure and domestic magazines. As Jenny McKay (2013) remarks: 'What most people immediately think about when magazines are mentioned are consumer publications, that is the ones which give readers information, advice and entertainment which relate to the time when they are not at work' (p. 26).

This is, of course, a wide definition. General entertainment titles are matched by those that aim to inform a more specialist (but non-professional) audience, such as those aimed at film buffs or car buyers. Although larger numbers of individual consumer magazines are sold in countries such as Japan and the USA, for its size the UK has a considerably diverse range of titles – approximately 3,000 consumer magazines, compared with 3,200 in the USA, a similar number despite having only a fifth of the population. However, this diversity brings its own problems, making the market much more competitive in the UK. Added to this, consumer titles have declined in circulation: the Advertising Association (www.adassoc.org.uk) listed sales at about 1.4 billion in 2004 compared with 2.1 billion in 1970, although this does include a slight increase from a low point of 1.2 billion in 1992.

Women's magazines

The most financially successful category of consumer magazines, women's magazines may not take up many of the top ten positions in terms of circulation (mainly filled by free subscription or supermarket magazines and TV guides), but they do dominate the lists of sold titles. Titles aimed at women only began to be produced more than a century after those for men, such as *The Tatler* and *The Gentleman's Magazine*, with publications such as the *Ladies' Home Journal* appearing in the mid-nineteenth century. It was during the twentieth century that these magazines exploded in circulation, becoming an attractive prospect for advertisers seeking to target the most active consumers in the home.

Today, BRAD lists 189 titles aimed primarily at women, although the categories are more diverse than the bestselling general lifestyle magazines, including 58 wedding and bride titles (such as *Wedding Journal* and *Asian Bride*), nine pregnancy and birth titles (*Baby & You*), 26 fashion and hair titles (*Boots Health & Beauty, Hair*), and ten professional and association titles (*Mslexia, WI Life*).

Of the best-selling monthlies aimed specifically at women in 2015, *Good Housekeeping* is one of the magazines once referred to as 'the Seven Sisters', titles aimed at married women and homemakers. While two of these ceased publication in the twenty-first century, and the circulation of the remaining five slipped (indicating in part just how much the market has changed since their heyday in post-war USA), *Good Housekeeping* in particular remains one of the highest-circulation magazines in the USA; published by Hearst Magazines, it contains information on food, relationships and fashion as well as, of course, the home.

Cosmopolitan, also from Hearst, is for many the classic women's magazine, although its focus on relationships, sex and careers belies some of the more investigative reporting of its earlier years; similar in look and feel are *Glamour* (Condé Nast) and *Marie Claire* (TimeInc. UK). *Yours* (Bauer Media Group, fortnightly), by contrast, taps into the growing prosperity of an older market, including features on pensions and celebrity interviews with performers as well as the more usual articles on health and beauty.

In addition to these titles, there is a huge market for women's weeklies. The traditional format, dominated by IPC's *Woman, Woman's Own* and *Woman's Weekly*, concentrated on home and family. The entry of *Bella* and *Closer* (Bauer) into the UK market in the late 1980s and 1990s brought a market shake-up with a stronger emphasis on gossip and chat, causing IPC to respond with the launch of *Chat*. Add to the mix celebrity news and entertainment, exemplified by *Hello!* (Hello Limited), *OK!* (Northern and Shell) and *Heat* (Bauer), and the weekly market became a hotly contested battleground.

As with much of the magazine market, women's titles have suffered deteriorating circulations in recent years, particularly in the weekly market. In some cases, these have been substantial (*OK!* lost 27.6 per cent of sales in the first

Figure 1.6 Alison Williams on the cover of *Glamour*. Image courtesy of Steve Pan/Glamour; © Condé Nast.

part of 2015 alone, for example), yet outside of celebrity gossip – which appears better catered for via online sites – the top ten selling weeklies still account for nearly four million magazines sold, with more traditional brands seeing losses of less than 5 per cent.

Men's magazines

For a long period it was felt that the market for general men's titles was moribund, the phrase 'men's magazines' being synonymous with soft-core pornography. This was despite the fact that men had bought magazines such as *Weekend* and *Tit-Bits* in their hundreds of thousands, and for more than the inevitable pin-ups that accompanied them.

Men's monthlies hit a high point in the late 1990s and early 2000s but have declined more substantially than women's titles in recent years, with only three brands – *Men's Health* (Hearst Magazines), *Forever Sports* (Haymarket) and *GQ* (Condé Nast) – remaining in the top 100. In recent years, the market for general men's titles has declined rapidly, and the era of the so-called 'lads' mags' appeared to come to an end in 2015 with the closure of the monthly *FHM* and the weekly *Zoo*. In many respects, the flourishing of men's titles – which proved extremely popular with advertisers even though sales never matched those for women's magazines – was a blip in the 1990s and early 2000s following the launch of *Loaded* in 1994, but stalwarts *Esquire* (founded in 1933) and *GQ* (whose original title, *Gentleman's Quarterly*, spoke of a more sophisticated audience in 1931), remain relatively popular.

In many respects, the men's magazine market has returned to the fragment-ation that applied prior to the 1990s, with titles abounding for specialist interests such as sports and hobbies, but even in more straightened times there remains a significant space for more general lifestyle magazines. *Men's Health*, which began life dealing entirely with health and fitness issues, has evolved into a more generalist title, covering technology, relationships and finance as well as the perfect way to develop abs (its usual lead story). At its height, the brand had a circulation of close to two million worldwide, and there remains a strong market for health and fashion titles, as well as more idiosyncratic offering such as *The Chap*, which 'seeks to reinstate such outmoded but indispensable gestures as hat doffing, giving up one's seat to a lady and regularly using a trouser press'.

B2B

While the largest circulating titles are aimed at general consumers, by far the largest number of publications consists of magazines aimed at specific professions, with nearly 5,000 titles in the UK according to BRAD. The B2B sector, which used to be known as trade magazines, largely consists of controlled circulation titles that are distributed directly to individuals and companies working in particular industries, although some are also sold on the newsstand. Examples include *Farmers Weekly* (Reed Business Information), *The Architects' Journal* (Emap) and *Press Gazette* (Progressive Media International).

While a substantial number of B2B titles are glossies that (in format if not content) look rather similar to consumer magazines, many also appear more like newspapers and some take the form of newsletters. A considerably greater number of B2B titles than consumer publications have also moved entirely online and, as well as demonstrating more diversity than the consumer sector in terms of the type of publications, the B2B market also tends to provide a great many other services to the businesses it serves, such as directories and conferences. As such, business and professional magazines are merely part of an information sector that is estimated to be worth £15.5 billion.

The big difference between business and consumer titles, of course, is that the audience for the former is much more tightly focused and, as such, publishers can charge much more per capita for advertising. For example, a popular general women's magazine such as *Cosmopolitan* can expect to charge between £13,000 to £23,000 per page of advertising depending on position with a circulation of a quarter of a million in the UK. By contrast, a specialist magazine for the aeronautics industry, *Flight International*, charges nearly £9,725 yet only has a worldwide circulation of approximately 31,000; the difference is that those readers include the chief executives of airlines and senior military staff who will be responsible for huge budgets.

The relationship with advertising in the B2B sector can be a difficult one because so many titles rely entirely on ads for revenue. At the same time, and this is particularly true for the top-circulating titles that are audited, the relationship with a professional readership requires a degree of trust and, indeed, the best B2B titles are often better in terms of their journalistic standards than a great many consumer magazines.

Staff working on business publications build up a degree of expertise in their field, and so often produce news stories and features that are comparable to the best newspaper publishing in the UK. Unfortunately, there are also plenty of trade titles that offer reviews that are little more than puff pieces for advertisers.

Because of the sheer diversity of the B2B sector, this book cannot hope to give a comprehensive guide to the market, but will offer a sample of three broad sectors: management and professional, trade and industry and medical.

Management and professional

Many large circulating B2B titles are general management publications such as *Business Network* (FSB Publications Ltd) and *Financial Management* (Guardian Media Group) that are aimed across a wide range of businesses, offering news and advice to those responsible for running and administrating companies in the UK. Other magazines concentrate much more on specific professions including accountancy (*Accounting and Business*, ACCA), the legal profession (*Law Society's Gazette*, the Law Society) and education (*Education Journal*, The Education Publishing Company Ltd).

While the majority of B2B publications will be released by commercial publishers, it is worth noting that a significant number of controlled circulation titles are also published and distributed by the professional bodies responsible for setting standards.

Trade and industry

Although professional titles tend to target a particular type of individual working in an organisation, there are also wider trade titles that provide an overview of an industry, including the motor trade (*Engine Repair and Remanufacture*, RGO Exhibitions & Publications Ltd), agriculture (*Farmer's Guardian*, Briefing Media), the grocery trade (*The Grocer*, William Reed) and computing (*The Computer Journal*, the British Computer Society).

Medical

Medical titles are, of course, professional and/or trade titles, the same as any other business publication. The reason for considering them separately is to demonstrate the significance of the NHS as one of the largest employers in Europe, which, in turn, generates a huge market for information at a range of levels. With more than 650 specialist titles available in the UK, these in turn break down into a wide range of specialist subcategories, including dentistry, cancer and oncology, sexual health and drug misuse, and even brands entirely devoted to medical equipment.

Contract publishing

The highest circulating magazines in the UK are not those bought on the newsstand by general consumers, but titles produced for companies such as Sky, the Automobile Association and the main supermarkets. In 2014, the title with the largest distribution was *The National Trust Magazine* (with more than two million subscriptions), followed by magazines for Asda and Tesco, with *TV Choice* the first fully paid-for title. Contract publishing (or custom publishing as it is also referred to) is a relatively new phenomenon in the UK, having only really taken hold when Redwood Publishing started business in the mid-1980s.

Most custom magazines are given away free. Contract publishing agencies also produce magazines, marketing materials and newsletters for corporations to be read by their customers or employees.

A feature that the larger custom titles share with other commercial publications is a tendency towards internationalisation. At the same time, these titles tend to be much more specialised than mainstream magazines, so that different versions will be tailored to different types of reader. Another distinction from general magazine publishing is that often the companies involved in contract publishing are also engaged in advertising, so that the relationship between editorial and advertising is much closer.

The largest contract publisher in the UK is John Brown Media (formed in 2002 by a merger between John Brown Publishing, previously responsible for *Viz* as well as a number of other consumer titles, and Citrus), with clients that include Waitrose and John Lewis. The company that revolutionised contract publishing, Redwood Publishing, was briefly controlled by BBC Magazines before coming under the control of the advertising agency Abbot Mead Vickers. It is very active internationally, for example, also being involved in selling advertising in the USA.

Partwork publishing

Partwork publishing is a rather specialist sector, particularly as the market is dominated by one publisher. A partwork is a series of magazines designed to be bound together as a complete book, usually accompanied by a free gift. Although the format is generally similar for such magazines (no advertising, building up information on a particular topic or extending information from simple to more complex subjects), the types of titles published are extremely varied and cover subjects such as computers, DIY, art, history and children's books.

The most important publisher, responsible for the majority of such titles in Europe and other parts of the globe as well as the UK, is De Agostini. An Italian company founded in 1901, it published its first partwork in 1959 (an Italian encyclopaedia). At any one time it will be publishing some 20 to 30 partwork magazines, each of which will appear in a limited number of issues before being completed.

News supplements

Newspaper magazines are distributed on Saturday and Sunday with the main UK newspapers, something that started in 1962 with the launch of the *Sunday Times Magazine*. Many of these are general interest supplements, combining some element of current affairs or reportage alongside leisure, sport, home, health and fashion articles, but an increasing number of titles also produce specialist magazines for sport or food. Indeed, while the glossy magazines tend to stand out from the rest of a newspaper, the tendency for the dailies and Sunday editions to be divided into sections for sport, reviews, technology, motoring and so on has led to what is commonly referred to as the 'magazinification' of newspapers.

As the circulations for the magazines as part of newspaper distributions are huge (nearly 1.5 million for the *Mail on Sunday*'s *YOU* magazine), these titles have an extremely significant readership base in the UK despite the relative decline of newspaper sales in the past decade, attracting considerable advertising revenue and also being able to dedicate resources to developing new markets.

Main publishers

H. Bauer: Established in Hamburg in 1875, H. Bauer Publishing claims to be the largest privately owned publisher in Europe, publishing 120 magazines in 13 countries. Its entry into the UK market was marked by the publication of *Bella* in 1987, with an emphasis on real-life stories, and again attracted attention in 1990 with the launch of *Take a Break*, with sales of over a million a week. It plays a major role in the women's and TV guide markets, making it one of the top three consumer publishers in the UK in terms of retail sales.

BBC Magazines: Part of the BBC's commercial services, BBC Magazines produces titles that are often (although not exclusively) linked to television programming for which it generates further revenue. The company concentrated on producing *Radio Times* and *The Listener* from the 1920s until the 1980s when it licensed *The Clothes Show* title and then extended its portfolio, primarily because of increased competition from TV listings magazines. It bought the company Redwood (which it later sold), and is now responsible for many top-selling consumer titles in the UK, including *Top Gear*, *Gardener's World* and *Focus*.

Condé Nast: A US-based publisher that specialises in upmarket publications and operates throughout Europe, the company was founded in 1909 when Condé Montrose Nast took over *Vogue*. The parent company is responsible for 18 publications, including the *New Yorker*, *GQ*, *Glamour* and *Condé Nast Traveller*.

Dennis Publishing: The largest UK independent publishing company (and often one of the most idiosyncratic due to the guiding principles of its founder, Felix Dennis, who was prosecuted in 1971 as co-editor of *Oz*), Dennis Publishing was founded in 1973 and gained an early success with *Kung-Fu Magazine*. In the late 1980s, *Computer Shopper* was the largest selling consumer IT title, while the 1990s saw the launch of *Maxim*, one of the highest circulating men's magazines in both the UK and the USA. It largely targets male readers, with other publications including *PC Pro*, *Poker Player* and the car magazines *Evo* and *Octane*.

Emap: Until late 2007, when it sold off its consumer titles and radio holdings, Emap was the second-largest publisher in the UK after IPC (now TimeInc. UK), having started out as a regional newspaper company in 1947. Now concentrating on B2B and professional networks, its key brands include *Retail Week* and *HSJ*.

Future: One of the largest magazine publishers in the UK, Future began in 1985 by producing computer magazines before expanding into other hobby and leisure interests. The company concentrates on niche markets such as general computer and gaming magazines, entertainment, sport and music, with titles such as *Edge*, *Total Film* and *T3*, and in recent years has begun closing many of its print offerings in favour of digital media.

Haymarket: Founded in 1957 as Cornmarket Press by Clive Labovitch and Michael Heseltine, the company became Haymarket in 1964 following investment by the printer Hazell Watson & Viney. Haymarket produces a number of popular consumer and B2B titles, as well as several tie-ins for the BBC such as *The Clothes Show*. It moved into the profitable medical market in the 1970s, and among its brands are *What Car?* and *PR Week*.

Hearst Magazines UK: Formed in 2011 from the merger of Natmag and Hachette Filipacchi UK, Hearst is now one of the leading publishers in the UK. Hearst Corporation, the American owner of Natmags, was established in 1910 and now has international editions of its titles in over 100 countries, producing some of the most high-profile consumer titles in the country, including *Cosmopolitan*, *Esquire* and *She*. Hachette was the UK subsidiary of Hachette Filipacchi Medias, itself a subsidiary of Legardère Media, one of the world's largest magazine publishers (and which began in Paris as a book publisher in 1826), best known in the UK for titles such as *Elle* and *Red*.

TimeInc. UK: The largest consumer publisher in the UK, and formerly IPC (International Publishing Company) until it became part of the Time Warner group in 2001. IPC was formed in 1963 from three magazine groups with roots extending back to the launch of *The Field* in 1853, while *Time* magazine was first published in 1923. It publishes more than 60 magazines across a diverse range of interests, including business and technology, food and wine, sport and fitness and travel. Its publications include *NME*, *Woman's Weekly* and *Wallpaper**.

The role of the Professional Publishers Association (PPA)

The Professional Publishers Association (PPA, www.ppa.co.uk) is the body responsible for magazine and professional media publishers in the UK, promoting and protecting the interests of the industry in general and its members (almost 400 companies) in particular.

The precursor of the PPA, the Society of Weekly Newspaper and Periodical Proprietors, was founded in 1913 under the chairmanship of Sir George Allardice Riddell. This, in turn, split into the Periodical, Trade Press and Weekly Newspaper Proprietors Association and the Newspaper Proprietors Association in 1941, although the combination of weekly newspapers and periodicals was short lived, leading to a separate Periodical Trade Press (PTP) association in 1942. By 1967, the various organisations had become the Periodical Publishers Association and this then changed its name to the Professional Publishers Association in 2010.

The aim of the PPA, as well as to act on behalf of the majority of companies in the UK, is to maintain professional publishing standards and, where possible, raise those standards to ensure a healthy industry. It achieves this in a number of ways: first, by running conferences, training courses and awards ceremonies to recognise best practice; second, by providing information via its web site and publications on issues such as legal matters and publishing procedures; and third, by working both with academic institutions to accredit courses and with publishing companies to provide specific training requirements.

As well as representing members that publish over 2,260 consumer and business titles, responsible for some 80 per cent of the UK market by turnover if not quantity of titles, the PPA also represents companies that produce directories and web sites, conferences, exhibitions and awards, as well as often having ties to broadcast media.

The PPA Editors' Code of Practice

Members of the PPA are encouraged to engage in best practice as part of upholding professional standards, including participating in ABC auditing to ensure that circulation figures are independently verified, and participating in self-regulatory arrangements.

In particular, the PPA Code covers the following, whereby members agree to:

- Maintain accuracy: the press will take care not to publish inaccurate, misleading or distorted content, including headlines not supported by the text.
- Respect privacy: the press will take care to respect the privacy of individuals and will need to justify intrusions into privacy made without consent.
- Not engage in harassment: this includes not telephoning, interviewing or photographing individuals once asked to desist.
- Respect special cases: journalists are expected to take additional care when reporting such things as suicides and children, especially those involved in cases of sexual abuse.
- Not use financial information for personal profit: this is especially important in financial journalism, and even where the law does not forbid it, journalists are not expected to use additional information for their own purposes.

A career in magazines

While choosing the appropriate degree (undergraduate or postgraduate) is increasingly the most important step in getting started on a career in magazines, it is not the only factor that the aspiring journalist should consider. Work experience, as with so many sectors of the media, is often crucial.

Because of the specialised and fragmentary nature of magazine publishing, the first thing to consider is your own interests, what your pastimes and hobbies are. Many graduates, at least in the early stages of study, tend to gravitate towards general men's and women's magazines, or general interest titles and supplements, but competition for these titles can be extremely severe. Working out where you will be able to engage your own interests with a more specialist consumer or B2B title is frequently a much better strategy for getting a work placement.

When applying with a CV, the PPA makes several useful recommendations, most notably that the variety of publications within the magazine industry make identikit applications extremely unhelpful. As such, the initial approach should indicate that you have undertaken some research into your target publication and market. At the very least, you should find the appropriate editor's name (consult the contact section of a title, as well as BRAD or *The Writers' and Artists' Yearbook*), but also where you will be able to fit your talents to a particular organisation – perhaps because an editor is due to go on holiday.

The PPA also observes that the ideal candidate would write like an angel, have a solid news- and features-based qualification, and an interest in the magazine topic since an early age, although in practice two out of three will lead to an interview. For further information to help you get started on a career in magazines, consult the PPA careers guide *Careers in Magazines and Business Media*, which covers publishing, sales, production and marketing as well as editorial and writing.

2
The business of magazines

This chapter will consider the structures of a 'typical' magazine company, by which is meant a commercial organisation whose main business is magazine production, whether consumer or B2B. However, this is by no means the only type of organisation involved in creating magazines: charities, religious groups, colleges and universities, businesses – all sorts of groups and individuals – may produce in-house or small-circulation titles. In addition, someone reading this book will presumably have a strong interest in producing their own title, perhaps for personal interest, but without necessarily being tied to a commercial publisher.

Indeed, even if attention is restricted to commercial magazine companies, the notion that there is a clear conventional structure runs into various difficulties. Some magazines are large operations with huge circulations and staffing levels to match, comprising a small to medium business in their own right; other titles, although happily turning a profit, may consist of a small team sharing responsibilities for editorial and design that would be divided more clearly in a larger company.

During the 1980s and 1990s, magazines began to refer to themselves as brands, reflecting the much more overtly commercial approach they took towards the business of publishing in comparison to newspapers. The prestige of national newspapers meant that in the post-war period some proprietors were willing (if not entirely happy) to run their journals at a loss because of their impact in politics and culture – Lord Thomson, for example, ran *The Times* at a considerable loss during the 1970s, and even the much cannier newspaper man Rupert Murdoch accepted a £266 million hit in 1991.

Circumstances have changed considerably in the intervening decades, particularly with regard to local and regional papers, but it still often goes against the grain for newspaper publishers and editors to describe their products as brands (though some, such as the *Guardian*, have taken to the term with aplomb). For those working on magazines, by contrast, the term has become thoroughly familiarised in the twenty-first century, especially as their content so often extends across digital platforms and even such things as events in addition to print.

The largest enterprises, such as Bauer, TimeInc. and Hearst Magazines, will have a managing director, president or chief executive officer, responsible ultimately for the business concerns and holdings of a media company as a whole. That particular role is far beyond the remit of this book; instead, the focus in this chapter will be on the role of the publisher and certain other related positions, such as advertising, marketing and administrative directors. While later chapters will turn to the roles of the editor and art editor, in this section I will also consider roles related to publishing such as directors of editorial strategy, something that often extends across the whole brand and not just a traditional print magazine.

The need to diversify has become particularly important in the past decade. While some titles have weathered the disruption caused by the 2008 crash well – *Vogue*, for example, had its most profitable year ever in 2015 – the market as a whole saw incredible disruption. The year that was the best ever for *Vogue* was also that in which the top-selling 100 magazine titles in the UK lost a combined 15 million from print circulation sales and some markets, most notably weekly celebrity magazines, have fallen away dramatically.

It is not all bad news by any means. In some respects, the painful transition has already taken place. For a long period many publishers continued as before, sure that readers would return to favoured brands. Having finally realised that would not happen, publishers such as Condé Nast and Hearst Magazines are pivoting their businesses, turning more to events, ecommerce and video to spice up their products.

The role of the publisher

Usually the most senior position on a magazine, the publisher is responsible for maintaining a brand's viability in commercial terms; that is, by promoting its visibility in the marketplace and ensuring that sufficient revenues are generated to keep a title in operation. As the majority of magazines rely on advertising for profitability, so publishers tend to rise through the ranks of advertising sales, although some may come from editorial or circulation backgrounds. Although the largest media companies will have a higher level of executive management above the level of publisher, in some smaller companies a publisher may be responsible directly for several titles and even be the proprietor of the company.

The publisher, then, can be considered the general manager of a title, responsible for its growth and success and, as such, has to be a strategist who pays attention not only to the business of magazines, but also with a wider eye on the general economy and conditions in the market. He or she will need to be aware of the types of audiences that are attractive to advertisers, as well as what readers are looking for from particular magazine markets (although this is much more of a concern for the editor in terms of day-to-day content).

Above all, the publisher needs to have a clear understanding of the 'mission' of a brand, its purpose and aims; ideally these are determined in conjunction with the editor and, in a company that produces a number of titles, will also need to be determined in line with a corporate overview of the publishing company's aims. However, in such circumstances, the publisher also needs to be the champion of the brand; in a drive to increase profitability, corporate management may frequently impose burdens on, or make changes to the mission of, a magazine that can generate revenues in the short term but are detrimental in the long term.

That said, however, a publisher always has to be interested in profit: without it, the vast majority of publications simply cease to exist, and while some journalists like to maintain a rather snooty attitude towards what they see as the filthy lucre of publishing – following a higher calling than mere advertising sales – there are very few journalists who are happy to pursue such a career without payment over the long term.

What is more, a publisher will also consider new ways to extend revenues through their understanding of the title as a core brand; a B2B publisher, for example, will probably look for opportunities to host conventions or trade shows related to their magazine mission. Some common ways of generating additional revenue include reprints or books (whether digital or print), custom publishing for advertisers or other clients, market research, and buyers' guides and catalogues, as well as conferences and seminars.

While the advertising sector – traditionally the main source of revenue for magazines – has seen a decline since the 2008 recession, there has been a growth in recent years of sponsored or 'branded' journalism (or, less frequently, 'corporate' journalism). In some respects, this is a repackaged variant of advertorial, whereby sponsors pay for content that is produced by staff on a particular title. Such branded content may be little more than barely declared advertising, and Sam Petulla (2014) makes a pretty convincing argument that branded journalism – in contrast to branded media – does not actually exist, in that proper journalism is not simply about a return on investment, and should maintain some distance from corporate ambitions.

Some titles, however, have taken brand journalism in interesting and innovative directions. Magazines such as *Forbes* and newspapers such as the *Guardian* are changing the nature of sponsored content; realising that what advertisers seek out most is an association with a trusted brand, they are not simply publishers for hire but instead produce material in a style that is immediately recognised by readers with much greater editorial independence and control.

The publisher and management

In addition to the strategic role in developing a magazine, the publisher is also often involved in departmental management – although how much he or she actually participates in day-to-day decisions and operations will vary depending on the size of a particular title. In smaller, one-title set-ups, the publisher will take a more direct approach to managing such things as circulation, digital strategy and marketing, as well as the general running of the office, but for larger companies he or she will delegate knowledgeable and experienced personnel to run different sections. In all cases, however, senior managers such as editors, strategy and advertising directors will report to the publisher.

At the opposite end of the scale to single-title publications are multiple-title organisations where functions may be centralised. This makes sense for a number of day-to-day tasks, such as human resources and accounting or financial planning, which will require similar procedures from one title to the next. Advertising and editorial are rarely centralised, although certain elements of production such as liaison with printers will benefit from being run out of a single location. The downside of centralisation can be that a publisher feels a lack of control (or responsibility) for areas outside his or her direct management.

The publisher and editorial

For a magazine to run successfully, the publisher will need to have an understanding of the ways in which different departments operate as a business. As has already been remarked, editorial will be dealt with in more detail elsewhere in this book, but it is worth bearing in mind how a publisher will typically organise the commercial running of his or her magazine.

In the vast majority of magazines other than those very few that are principally read as advertising catalogues, or promotional titles for 'hot' new products, editorial pages are key to commercial success. Consumers purchase titles to read features, reviews and news, and while the role of advertising should not be underestimated (in that a great deal of information other than simple consumer decisions can be gleaned from adverts), material produced by journalists and designers will be essential to making or breaking a magazine.

For the publisher, then, editorial is a major cost centre but an essential one: certainly for the editor it must seem that all other aspects of publishing are ultimately geared towards ensuring the continued growth and success of the content he or she is responsible for.

Conflicts and agreement

While some publishers like to have a more hands-on approach to editorial, it is a rare magazine where this produces harmonious results. The setting up of a separate editorial fiefdom, however, is unlikely to be efficient. The publisher's role, then, is not to manage the writing, photography, layout and design of a magazine, but more to ensure that editorial principles are in line with the overall intentions and functions of a title and publishing company.

Publisher and editor should be in agreement as to the aims and intentions of the brand, and very often in larger companies the publisher serves as a buffer between corporate management and the editor and also in the tricky relationship between editorial and advertising. Frequently, publishing houses will have policies in place to ensure that there is a proper procedure for maintaining relations between editorial and sales, the latter notoriously interested in influencing what appears in the former, as good reviews or product placements can make their job much easier although being seen as a soft touch for advertisers can be detrimental to the long-term interests of a magazine. In some cases, there may even be a policy of separation between those departments.

Although publishers are unlikely to have come from a writing background, their knowledge of the market should make them good readers and there are plenty of publishers who are avid consumers of competitor titles. This, in turn, can make them an important sounding board for editorial decisions. The publisher will also have an essential role to play in legal issues that may arise from editorial, having responsibilities with the editor concerning libel, for example. Finally, an editor will have to discuss and arrange budgets in conjunction with the publisher.

Advertising and media sales

For the vast majority of magazines, advertising has long been the key to financial success and, therefore, is an area that deeply involves publishers, so much so that the publisher is also sometimes the advertising director on smaller magazines.

As with all print media, magazine advertising has been affected by the economic downturn since 2008, in some countries more noticeably than others. According to the McKinsey Global Media Report for 2014, while the total spend for all media across the world rose from $1.2 trillion in 2008 to just over $1.6 (after a dip in 2009–10), for print consumer magazines the total spend fell from $78 billion to $64 billion.

That is far from the final picture, however. Many of the massive increases have come in digital advertising (which McKinsey estimated to double from nearly $1.25 billion in 2013 to just below $2.5 billion by 2018), and this emphasises just how important digital strategies have become to the most successful brands. Indeed, as Arif Durrani (2015) reported from the PPA Festival many publishers were feeling optimistic about the future for the first time in a decade.

While events, ecommerce and hosting content offer new opportunities to brands, advertising remains as important as ever. Certainly a key role for any publisher is to help build relations with the most important advertising clients, and to ensure that a title provides a suitable environment which will be appealing to them.

For example, just about every market has important advertisers who are also competitors, and if a title is seen to give preferential treatment to one over another this can generate negative reactions; one area that can be extremely significant in this regard is when placing adverts on prime spots in a title, such as the inside front or back covers, or nearer the front of a magazine. Because of this, publishers have to put in place a clear policy that will explain why such decisions are made. Likewise, many brands will allow advertisers to capture the home page of their web sites, thus attracting much more attention from visitors – which, again, has to be handled sensitively with regard to all the other potential advertisers on the site.

In addition, a good publisher will want to be seen as an important figure in the industry of which his or her magazine is a part. Liaising with clients (who may also be advertisers) involves attending conferences, trade shows and any other important event where the profile of a title can be raised, and to which he or she can make a contribution in terms of expertise and knowledge.

Over a little more than a hundred years, magazines have become extremely successful vehicles for advertising, but they are just one platform – even within the same brands themselves. When selling space in a print magazine or on a web site, the advertising director along with the publisher must consider what alternatives may be open, such as television and social media as well as other competing titles, and the purpose of a campaign.

Advertisers will have a particular audience that they wish to reach, and sometimes a campaign will be seasonal, such as in the run-up to Christmas. Sales teams will wish to consider the strategy for when they approach advertisers as well as the reasons why their title will be more appealing.

Advertisers, agencies and sales teams

The advertising director will have a responsibility to research the market, to know companies and their products in order to discover which are more suitable than others. A consumer IT title, for example, will bring little benefit to manufacturers or service providers who are mainly responsible for supplying large companies.

Market segmentation is often extremely important; some advertisers divide potential consumers along demographic lines such as age or income, while others see occupational categories as more important. Of course, the success of previous advertising campaigns (particularly ones which drew positive responses from the publisher's own title) needs to be kept in mind.

Nearly all advertising – certainly large-scale campaigns by national or international companies – is run through advertising agencies, and it is usually these that a sales team will be dealing with. Approaching a producer directly can be counter-productive, not merely because a company will have hired such an agency to provide expertise, but because this can be seen to be going behind the agency's back; fairly understandably, they will not be inclined to place any of their other clients in a title that engages in what they see as sharp practice.

One other factor facing magazine publishers is whether to have an in-house media sales team or to use a third-party sales agency. An in-house team has the advantage of knowing the magazine in much more detail and providing full control to the publisher, but has the disadvantage of higher costs and requiring greater management.

Using an agency can provide a possible existing customer base for new publications, and is a resource that can be used as and when required – but is also unlikely ever to know as much about the magazine as a media sales team that can be trained and build up experience over time. Where centralisation does tend to occur, it is often in large publishing companies that offer media sales over their own stable of titles.

Advertising departments

How large an advertising department is depends on the number of pages of advertising that are sold and the volume of advertising revenue. Most titles cannot survive on circulation revenues alone – and for controlled circulation magazines that do not charge a cover price their income is usually entirely dependent on media sales.

In the UK, as opposed to the USA, it is unusual for a sales director to also have regional directors, but he or she will often be responsible for a number of account managers, each of whom has responsibility for particular clients or areas of media sales within a magazine. In the very smallest titles, the sales director may even be the publisher working with one or two sales staff.

The advertising manager or director will be responsible for providing estimates of revenue as well as devising a sales strategy (in conjunction with the publisher), part of which will involve developing relations with advertisers and their agencies. Providing realistic estimates is important because it will determine the level of spending throughout all levels of a magazine and so, of course, influence a title's profit or loss.

Part of the sales strategy includes taking into account short-term economic conditions, but also paying attention to the market in which a brand operates. In doing this, the sales manager will need to understand why current advertisers buy space in the title for which he or she works, and why similar advertisers do not – and what can be done to bring them on board.

While some brands maintain a more or less strict division between sales and editorial, to work out this strategy effectively requires cooperation between him or her and the editor. Finally, he or she will also have responsibilities for the sales team (including hiring and firing) and for the department budget.

Media sales

Someone working in media sales will be given responsibility for a number of accounts, involving establishing and maintaining relationships with clients and their agencies, representing the magazine and closing sales. A main task of an account manager is to make sales calls, either to set up initial meetings or follow up, all of which build the rapport between an advertiser or potential advertiser and the magazine.

The task for someone working in sales is to get to see an advertiser in what will often be a busy schedule; such meetings are often accompanied by a formal or informal presentation in which a pitch will be made explaining what the benefits are for an advertiser to buy space in the magazine.

Account managers will also often have to send through technical or legal material (such as page sizes for adverts, schedules and contracts), and nearly every medium- to large-scale title will run some form of customer relationship management (CRM) system, a database in which contact details and information on sales are stored, and which members of a team are meant to update on a regular basis.

Once he or she has made contact with a client and their agency, a sales representative must maintain regular contact, and an important role is played by entertainment, such as lunch or evening events; for dedicated sales people in the media business, this is rarely a nine to five job. As well as building up knowledge of the brand itself, such a person must also learn about the needs of a client. Members of a sales team will be expected to communicate news about the magazine in a useful way and get to know different people working in clients' markets.

As with many such jobs, media sales can bring a considerable amount of stress and the churn rate of hiring and firing can be fairly high (certainly much higher than editorial). Payment packages are almost invariably in the form of a basic salary plus bonuses for what are called over target earnings (OTE): if your allotted space to sell is to bring in ten advertisers for print and digital formats, and you meet that target, then you will receive your basic salary, but increasing that amount can improve earnings significantly.

Ad placement

Agencies can place advertisements in a magazine in a variety of ways. The most common form is display advertising, usually a single page or double-page spread (DPS), although there are plenty of titles that offer display advertising that can take up a fraction of a page such as a half or quarter and some that will offer a gatefold, a page that folds out. This is usually glossy and full colour, although some magazines will offer full-page black and white ads if they do not print throughout in colour.

Different formats have emerged for online display advertising. A leaderboard ad is a wide, rectangular banner, typically at the top of the page and is probably what most people think of for online adverts. A mid-page unit (MPU) is a specified box, 300 x 250 pixels in size that can appear anywhere in the page, while a half-page unit (HPU) is a larger banner ad that typically runs down the side of a page. At their simplest, these will be images that appear on the page, but some brands allow advertisers to 'skin' their sites or particular pages with a backdrop image, and of course animation and even some interactivity such as a game can attract visitors' attention. Skins, along with rollbacks or cascades – where the advert rolls out to fill a page – are more expensive that typical banners.

Online advertising costs are usually charged per thousand page views, also known as cost per mille (from the French word for thousand, CPM). For those with cash to burn, the most dramatic option offered by a view sites is a homepage takeover, replacing the front page of a web site with the advertiser's message. To give an example of the relative costs, ElleUK.com begins at a very reasonable £45 CPM rising to £45,000 per week for a homepage takeover.

An entirely new market that has emerged in the past decade is social media advertising. Rather than bookmarking their favourite brands, more and more readers come to articles through links on sites such as Facebook, Twitter and LinkedIn. One particular appeal of social media advertising is that, in contrast to normal web advertising, users are much more likely to click through on a link so that the click through rate (CTR) can be anything up to nine times higher. As no major media brands control the most popular social media platforms, however, this is something that they have to pay to use as with any other advertiser.

Another common format is classified, which, as with newspapers, can range from a few lines costing a few pounds to more usual boxouts with small images and contact information, or even occasionally full-page ads. While classified advertising is typically much cheaper than display ads, for some brands this can be a very profitable enterprise; charging tens or hundreds of pounds can make a single page of space more lucrative than a single page of display advertising.

Where advertisements are placed in a print magazine or on a web site can have a major impact on how they are received by the reader. It is for this reason that many (though not all) titles charge more depending on where an advert appears. To appear on the back or inside covers, or to take over the homepage or skin a site, is a premium position that will cost most, while many titles charge more for ads placed near the front third or quarter or near the top of a web page than for those appearing near the back or lower down on a screen. In addition to placement, publishers will often try to 'lock in' an advertiser for as long as possible, and the easiest way to do this is to offer a discount for ads that are taken out over more than one issue.

Rate cards

Because costs can vary according to position, important information that publishers offer to prospective advertisers as part of a media pack (covered in more detail in the next chapter) is in the form of a rate card. This will list information such as the cost for full-page and DPS advertising, different web formats depending on whether they are MPUs or banners, factoring in such things as discounts for a series of ads over three, six or 12 months.

In addition, a magazine will be required to state the terms and conditions of the contract between it and an advertiser, such as the consequences of cancelling an advert, who is responsible for accuracy and payment. Also, the advertiser will have a strong interest in the number of copies a title sells, which will be considered under auditing in the next chapter.

Wherever possible, a publisher will try to move a title towards a rate card, a clear set of prices that he or she believes the market can afford. Difficulty often occurs if a particular industry is going through troubled times; at such moments, publishers may lose money because advertisers tighten their belts and do not spend as much on ad campaigns – something that very evidently happened in a wide range of sectors in 2009–10, although as already noted the market has been improving again in more recent years.

The danger that can ensue when haggling over prices is that if an agency discovers that a competitor has preferential rates that are not transparent (that is, included on the rate card), it may also seek to negotiate its own discounts and a magazine is soon caught in a vicious circle where all its advertisers seek to pay less than the going rate. During a downturn publishers may decide to lose advertising rather than cut their rate card, gambling that when the market improves clients will return at the full rate.

Advertising

The conventional and liberal view of the effects of advertising is that consumers are rational buyers who effectively know what is best for them. In relation to this, they make independent and informed choices and it is the task of the advertiser to ensure that they receive the most appropriate information to help them make that choice. This certainly is the opinion of organisations such as the Advertising Standards Agency, which sees its role as to ensure that they will not be misled by false advertising – and which can insist that such ads are removed and fines levied on those who create them.

Against this view is one that developed from post-Marxist cultural traditions, which points out that branding relies on fantasy and that compulsive buying indicates irrational reactions on the part of the consumer. In addition, following Bourdieu (1986), the notion that we are clear-thinking, rational consumers has to take into account such things as family socialisation and education, which determine the taste for a wide range of goods. What Bourdieu calls

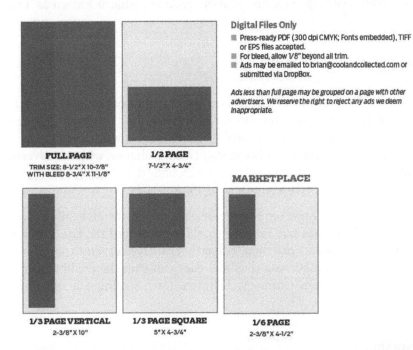

Figure 2.1 A typical advertising rate card from *Cool & Collected*

'cultural capital' comes (among other things) from the ways in which we are judged according to our taste – and, in turn, we are what we buy.

For magazines, the relationship is rarely this vexed in terms of building a readership – successful editors realise that they depend on media sales for the continued existence of their titles (and their jobs), but problems can arise in terms of the role of maintaining editorial independence from advertisers.

The relationships developed in magazines are triangular, between the staff producing titles, their readers and the advertisers. The importance of magazines to the latter is that they deliver potential consumers who will buy their products, but to maintain a high circulation (and thus those potential consumers) depends on trust existing between editorial and the audience; if a magazine is seen to be straying too close to its advertisers, for example, by delivering reviews that are seen as not independent, it can too easily lose readers.

The ways in which this delicate relationship is sometimes developed can be seen by three attempts to reach readers via other means than direct advertising, such as 'advertorials', sponsorship or, more recently, what is known as 'brand journalism'.

Advertorials

Advertorial is usually indicated in a magazine or newspaper by a phrase such as 'advertising special feature', and is material produced by a company to promote their products that looks like a normal feature in the title in which it appears. It will typically be written by in-house staff (in consultation with the advertiser or its agency), and is justified usually on the grounds that it provides something 'extra' for the reader in terms of providing information.

The question remains, however, whether it is acceptable for ads to 'do' editorial; certainly, advertorial was rare in quality publications until the late 1990s, but has been gaining ground since then. Advertisers are often keen to pay more for this type of promotion because they feel they can gain the credibility of the title, but although often extremely lucrative for a magazine it can also be damaging if pursued too far.

Sponsorship

Sponsorship is another route taken to avoid direct advertising, and has long been accepted as part of the commercial background for most commercial magazines as well as other media. Sponsors (or editors) can emphasise the separation between magazine and advertiser by issuing a separate supplement, or indicate a closer relationship by running regularly sponsored pages, such as a competition page or particular section of a web site. The phrase 'in relation with' usually indicates that the sponsor has some say in the final appearance of the page or product, while 'sponsored by' tends to mean that the advertiser simply wishes to gain prestige from an association with a brand, with content being editorially driven.

While the links between editorial and advertising can sometimes be strained, with the latter seeking to influence the former, there is one important area in which they must be developed if a title is to have any hope of being successful. The editor must keep constant links with the advertising team to let them know what features and stories will be appearing in future issues. With advance knowledge of the editorial calendar – which will be available to the entire magazine staff and, indeed, to external sources as well – the sales team can start to target potential contacts who may be willing to advertise in a particular issue that they know is covering subjects pertinent to their business.

Brand journalism

Despite having been a common phrase only in recent years, the notion of 'brand journalism' is already contention enough for commentators to argue that it does not (or should not) exist. In contrast to advertorial, which is clearly designed to sell a product or service, brand journalism – as the name suggests – is journalism that is undertaken for a brand or organisation, sometimes with the intention of selling goods but at other times dedicated to raising awareness of specific issues. Thus a group such as Amnesty International works with publishers to sell books on human rights, just as HSBC publishes a Global Connections magazine.

From the early 2000s, many companies found that the power of the web meant they could connect directly with consumers, but also that they lacked the experience that more traditional publishers had when it came to getting their message across effectively. As such, journalists are often employed to create those stories, contracted and employed through publishers and agencies, to write stories that will raise brand awareness or supplement the work of mainstream media.

There are several examples of best practice that have been publicised by brands such as *Forbes* magazine, which led the way on brand journalism. Thus, for example, it is extremely important to be transparent about the connections between a publisher and the brand they are working for. Should the facts emerge – and it is only a question of when rather than if – that will cause considerable damage for the reputation of all parties involved. Likewise, simply writing ad copy will be discovered quickly by readers and discarded as such. As such, when producing brand journalism it is as important to maintain as objective and truthful a stance as possible.

Of course, this does not address the main concerns of detractors – that the very term 'brand journalism' is an oxymoron, reducing the independence of journalists that is essential to their craft. At its very best, however, companies and organisations want to hire successful media companies because they want to be associated with that brand and, as such, to interfere too much will result in copy that does not carry the authentic feel of that publisher.

Marketing and promotion

Along with sales, another area that a publisher often has direct involvement with is marketing and promotion. Just as a title has to attract advertising investment to survive, so it also has to sell itself to make sure that it is as prominent as possible in the marketplace.

Larger magazines may have a dedicated marketing manager, or a marketing department that operates over several titles, but for smaller publications it may be that the publisher takes direct responsibility for promoting his or her title. Whoever is in charge, the task for marketing and promotion is to ensure that a definite brand is in the reader's mind when he or she goes out to buy a magazine.

In contrast to newspapers, where despite declining circulations (often a result of increasing cover prices) readers will often remain loyal to their particular national or local daily or weekly newspaper or web site, rarely if ever buying the competition, magazine readers – at least for consumer titles – are notoriously promiscuous. Someone who buys *Bella* one week might try out *Take a Break* in another, or go for a monthly such as *Glamour*.

In addition, certain types of magazines are seasonal in their sales: readers tend not to buy wedding titles every month of the year – or indeed, very often at all during their lives; in the months prior to a marriage, however, consumers may purchase a large number of competing titles for advice and tips in the run-up to the big day. What the marketing department will seek to do is ensure that, as much as possible, readers (and also advertisers) are aware of its title in the heavily competitive environment of the newsstand and the web.

In addition to promoting the magazine, a marketing manager will often work in conjunction with the circulation department to find out what the readers want and think of a magazine, and in this respect can provide valuable information to the editorial department as well as the publisher. This may take the form of research via questionnaires within a title, phone polls or even focus groups, where ideas can be tested out with a smaller group of individuals.

Promotion can include advertising, for example on television, billboards or through social media, to draw the public's attention to a new launch or changes that have been made to an old favourite; TV advertising is very rare for all but the largest general consumer titles, not merely because it is so expensive but also because most magazines have target markets that are very specific, and so will waste money appealing to a large television audience. Social media has also become an important aspect for promoting a brand, both in the form of advertising but also engaging in more varied strategies through Twitter, Facebook and others.

For multi-title companies, advertising might also take place across related magazines and web sites owned by the same company. However, for titles with smaller revenues or with very focused audiences, such as controlled circulation B2B magazines, advertising might be dispensed with altogether. This does not mean, however, that other forms of promotion can be neglected.

Promotional materials and public relations

One very common way of promoting a brand to advertisers in particular is via media packs. These will be covered in more detail in the next chapter, but they are designed to help strengthen a magazine as a brand, positioning it in the market and indicating such things as the typical reader and audience, as well as providing useful information on advertising rates and technical information (such as page sizes) for advertisers providing electronic files.

Although television advertising can be seen as a waste of money, point-of-sale materials, while expensive, can be extremely useful in attracting the consumer's attention at the newsstand. These can include display cases that make a title stand out from the competition, and for which a newsagent will charge a premium, to cover mounts offering 'free' gifts to the reader.

While advertisers will often approach magazines requesting information such as media packs (or, increasingly, use the web), publishers will also maintain promotion lists for direct mailing. Similar lists will be used to target readers, but the big challenge lies in making such promotional materials interesting enough to appeal to an audience, whether attracting new readers to a magazine or sparking interest in advertising, so that the promotional materials will not be discarded immediately as junk mail. To this end, a common tactic when appealing to readers is to link promotional materials to competitions which may or may not come through sponsorship.

A main point of liaison between a marketing manager and the editorial team comes from writing press releases. The purpose of such releases is to try to get stories and features covered in a title into the local or national press, radio or television. During the planning stage, an effective editor will alert the marketing department as to any potentially interesting stories, and they or one of their team may even be involved in the writing of press releases that are sent out.

Likewise, a marketing team will look for opportunities to promote a title by getting members of staff to appear in the media when a story breaks on which they can offer an authoritative perspective. This is something that is particularly important to the B2B market, where the role of experienced journalists as pundits helps improve the prestige of the magazine – as well as providing expert information for news and feature stories.

The role of PR

PR plays an important role in magazines – usually because editors and journalists are on the receiving end of information and events provided by public relations companies. However, because a magazine's standing is important within the industry, many titles use PR techniques themselves to improve their relationships with advertisers and customers.

New titles will wish to create a buzz and spread the word that this is a magazine worth watching, while older brands will want to reiterate that they are market leaders in the field. To this end, as well as sending out press releases a marketing department may organise parties for such things as anniversaries or new launches, as well as sponsor events related to the magazine's core business.

When useful (or favourable) articles appear in a magazine, it is not unusual for advertisers to seek to use these in their own promotions, and so a marketing manager and publisher should have a policy on reprints or, more typically, duplicating content on an advertiser's web site, determining when and where copyrighted material from the title can appear and how much it costs to re-use in this way. For the advertiser, having won plaudits from a respectable title can be a way of improving its own standing, but sometimes companies may approach a magazine seeking to use information that is not directly related to one of their goods but offers information that they see as being useful to their customers.

Related to this is the potential for market research. A marketing department may often seek to generate information for its own uses by contacting readers and will also build up industry expertise through its editorial staff. As has already been noted when discussing different market sectors, B2B titles will often be involved in additional activities such as conferences and trade shows, and these can often be integral to the success of a title.

Such research can, for many titles of a specialist nature, move beyond simple promotion of the magazine and become the development of an industry, writing white papers for companies, for example, that bring together the fruits of research by various bodies.

Administration

Of the remaining departments that the publisher has ultimate responsibility for, the duties of a circulation manager and the principles of distributing a title are the subject of the next chapter. One area that he or she has to consider, however, is the general office management for the title, including maintaining a reception and communications facilities for visitors to the title or others who may wish to get in touch, organising meetings between various departments within a magazine and also external bodies, such as insurers, legal firms or accountants.

The magazine budget

The largest costs for a publisher are staff salaries and add-on costs (such as pension contributions) and production, including printing, paper and binding. Desktop publishing has brought down some costs by making it possible to take control of functions such as layout and design that were once undertaken by third parties, and advances in pre-press preparation such as the ability to print to plate have also brought savings, but at the same time a magazine has to invest in hardware and software in-house.

Paper and printing remain major costs and the relationship between a publisher and its printer is extremely important. For large titles with high-volume distributions, changing printers is not something undertaken lightly. Likewise, paper costs have to be constantly monitored. While digital distribution is considerably cheaper than for print, this can still be a huge resource not just in terms of staffing but also to ensure that a web site is available 24 hours a day, 365 days a year.

Underlying these and other such activities is the financial management of a title, for which the publisher is responsible. If this is a single title, the publisher may also be the owner and so the financial health of his or her title can be a more personal concern; but even someone employed by a company will have a strong interest in the debt, cash and capital of the brand.

As well as profit or loss, he or she will have to pay attention to cash flows and investors; as well as changes 'internal' to the magazine that may affect profitability, such as declining circulation or advertising, the publisher will need to pay attention to 'external' factors that could lead to an economic downturn and so affect a publisher as well as other sectors of the economy. If the year ahead looks poor, then budgets need to be arranged accordingly, otherwise there will be a potential disaster later on if revenues fall below budget and redundancies have to be made.

When preparing the budget for a magazine, whether a new title or ongoing financial planning, the publisher needs to take into account the following factors:

- The number of advertising pages or units, including display and classified as well as special digital promotions such as homepage takeovers, which will give an estimate of ad revenues for the year compared with the proposed rate card.
- Circulation estimates: on paid-for magazines, this will provide additional revenues from newsstand sales and subscriptions. For digital, this will include the number of page views for a web site or downloads of digital editions.
- Total number of editorial content as well as advertising pages. An increase in both editorial and advertising will, of course, bring with it greater pro-duction costs for print (including physical distribution) and digital, although an increase in advertising pages also increases revenue.
- The print run; that is, how many copies of the magazine will be printed. This can provide a basic estimate of mechanical costs for printing, binding and distribution.
- The editorial/advertising (ed/ad) ratio; that is, the percentage of editorial pages printed against advertising ones. A magazine will have a target ratio, such as 70 per cent editorial to 30 per cent advertising; too much editorial will increase costs, but too little will make the title less appealing to readers.
- Staffing costs, including direct costs such as salaries and benefits, and other costs such as expenses.
- Other administrative and business overheads, such as insurance, rent, depreciation and repairs and maintenance.

With these figures, it is possible to work out a profit and loss record – how much the magazine needs to earn to break even or go into profit. At the same time, while the budget tends to be set annually, the financial status of the magazine has to be monitored on a regular basis. So sales and circulation figures have to be compared to projections made in the annual budget to see whether revisions have to be made for the rest of the year.

Obviously, in most instances publishers are looking for any warning signs that they might not be hitting targets, but occasionally a lucky publisher may find themselves in a position where they go over target – which can bring its own problems: the proprietors of a magazine, when the market is in a good economic position, will expect growth year on year. If for some reason a title is particularly successful in one year, this may raise unrealistic expectations for subsequent budgets, so the publisher may wish to make additional capital expenditures in a particularly profitable year to manage those future expectations.

As the review of budgets is important to the ongoing health of a title, it is usual that such meetings will take place on a monthly basis and be attended by the publisher, sales director and editor at least, along with any other managers on the magazine such as circulation directors and marketing managers where appropriate. The function of such a meeting, as well as reviewing what has happened previously, should be to remind those managers of the importance of remaining in control of their expenses and also seek to provide useful ideas for future developments.

Financing a new title or acquisition

For publishers seeking to start up a new title, whether as a first step into publishing or as part of business expansion that may also include acquisition of a competitor's magazines, the question of finding enough capital to finance the operation is the most important one.

The first step is to prepare a business plan, typically consisting of the following sections:

- An executive summary that states what you want from the business – who your audience will be, how you hope to establish a profitable title in the marketplace and what you are looking for in terms of investment.
- A description of the industry you will be working for – for example, a particular professional sector if you are launching a B2B title, as well as the operations for producing and distributing a magazine, a digital strategy for getting to readers on the web or through mobile, how it will be sold and also any legal forms, whether this is sole proprietorship, a partnership or part of a corporation.
- A market analysis, indicating why there might be an audience for this type of magazine and, ideally, the results of research carried out to discover what type of magazine proposed readers would be looking for.
- A competitive analysis that outlines other players in this particular field and provides an account of how this new title will be different and why it is needed.

- An account of how the business will be run – for example, the structure of editorial, sales and circulation departments outlined in this and the next chapter – and how it will develop. For example, if the market for one type of magazine typically sustains sales of 50,000 copies sold on the newsstand and/or by subscription per year, you would need to indicate how you would achieve similar distributions. In addition, potential investors would want to know what plans there are to develop the business for future growth. As such, a design and development plan would need to deal with product, market and organisation development.
- Financial data, outlining the expenses and capital requirements. The elements outlined in the preceding section on magazine budgets would need to be analysed here, to demonstrate how much you think it would cost to run a magazine and what projections for income would be.

At all stages, independent legal and financial advice is always recommended, providing a perspective on what is feasible for a new launch or acquisition. The options then open to many publishers include:

- Senior debt finance: traditional secured bank loans, typically short term and paid back from a company's cash flow over three to five years.
- Venture capital or private equity: the investor takes a stake in the equity of the firm in return for the initial cash investment. Future earnings rather than current cash flow will repay the debt, and the investor will usually seek to recoup costs through selling the business or a stock-market flotation.
- Internal investment: for large publishers, part of the profits from other operations are used to launch new titles, and in some cases a title may change owners due to such things as a senior management buyout.
- Government-backed finance: this can consist of grants or small firms loans that are often extremely useful for very small operations, and banks are able to advise on the various grants and loans currently available throughout the European Union.

When approaching potential investors, a major concern will not just be the product itself and the possibilities of growth, but also the strength of a management team. If at some stage a publisher wishes to sell or buy a title, then they should also employ a broker who is knowledgeable about the magazine market (details for which can be found via the PPA) to evaluate properly the value of a title and negotiate any deals, a tax accountant to ensure that they can take full advantage of tax breaks and a commercial lawyer with media experience.

Auditing and sales verification

As well as gaining the finance to launch a title, a publisher will also need to consider how copies of sales are recorded. Until advertising became important for generating revenue, there was no attempt to verify how many copies of a particular magazine were sold. The Audit Bureau of Circulations (ABC, www. abc.org.uk) was founded in 1914 and the Business Publications Audit, Inc. (BPA, www.bpaww.com) in 1931; each was set up by groups of advertisers and publishers to provide an impartial and external mechanism that would audit magazine sales and standardise how information was presented.

Both of these companies perform a similar function, the main difference being that while ABC has a much larger membership overall, BPA has traditionally performed more strongly in the business sector. The classification systems used by each company were merged in the mid-1980s, making it easier to compare results across both.

Circulation is initially reported in a publisher's statement (in the USA referred to as a 'pink sheet'), the best estimate of sales in a six-month period from January to June, or July to December. Auditors then analyse that statement for accuracy and issue their own report. The importance of this process is that it helps advertisers determine not only the number of copies sold, but also if the manner in which they are sold meets their expectations. For example, if an advertiser deals only in the UK, then if large numbers of a title are sold abroad this may affect how they deal with a magazine. It is also worth noting that magazine circulation is very different to a magazine's audience which will usually be much larger, the assumption being that more than one person reads each copy.

A circulation statement contains information on average paid circulation, from the newsstand for print and digital single-sale copies and subscriptions (including sponsored subscriptions, that is quantities of 11 or more), and non-paid circulation. In addition to the controlled circulation discussed previously, this can include consumer titles that send out copies or allow the download of a magazine at no charge to public places or individuals with an affiliated interest.

Over a six-month period, this then produces the total average circulation, the number of copies sold in total divided by the number of issues over that period. ABC has particular rules about which copies can be included; for example, a publisher must provide information about where the magazine will be sold, as well as analysis of individual subscriptions. In addition, the publisher must provide a reader with the opportunity to opt out of a subscription – a reflection of the fact that unscrupulous publishers can inflate their circulation figures by sending out free copies that a reader no longer requires.

Creating a media pack

A media pack is aimed principally at advertisers and potential investors in a title, and typically provides the following information:

- Editorial statement: this will also often be referred to as a brand statement, and is intended to provide a concise view of the magazine's status, ambitions and purpose. Sometimes this will include a brief outline of the typical content of an issue or recent features, as well as seeking to position the title in terms of an editorial stance (for example, whether it is combative, investigative, informative, the reader's friend and so on). In attempting to outline the aims and ambitions that establish the core brand, this is the opportunity to establish what may be distinctive about a particular title.

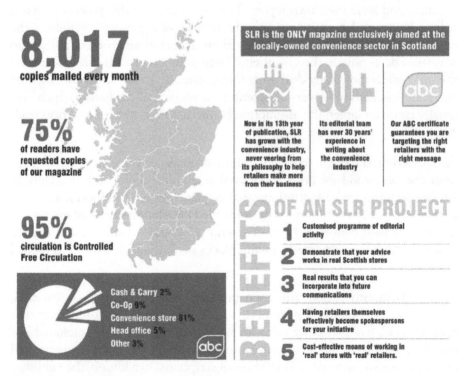

Figure 2.2 SLR Magazine media pack

- Market and readership: in seeking to attract potential advertisers, a media pack often includes demographic information (age, gender, socioeconomic status) and details specific to a particular group (for example, if they share an interest in urban music, are women in their twenties or are an audience largely comprising flight professionals). In some cases, a media pack may refer to competitors in the field (although usually only in the vaguest terms) to indicate what is different about this particular title.

- Verified/estimated circulation: as has already been established, the significance of auditing is that it verifies circulation, but some smaller titles that cannot afford or choose not to go down the auditing route may offer estimated circulation figures. Media packs will also often distinguish between paid circulation and readership, the latter usually being between two to four times the size of the former (the assumption being that a magazine will be passed around after it is bought).

- Advertising rates: one of the principal functions of a media pack is to provide information on advertising costs, which will normally be provided in the form of a rate card. At its simplest, this will break down ad rates based on size (so that a DPS is more expensive than a single page of display advertising which, in turn, costs more than a half page and so on), but larger titles will also typically have a more complex set of prices. Position is important, so that adverts near the front of a magazine, or those facing suitable editorial content (facing matter), cost more than those towards the end, with the most expensive rates reserved for inside or back covers. In addition, some titles will offer discounts on advertising that is bought over a longer period.

- Additional information: while editorial and advertising material tends to be common to all media packs, sometimes they may include additional information on such things as distribution (if a title is distributed via special arrangements, such as through particular shops or trade shows, or subscriptions), online versions which are becoming particularly important to magazine publishers, research or other business services which are especially significant to the B2B sector, as well as links to trade shows, conferences or syndication rights.

3
From print to mobile

The digital revolution

The biggest transformation that has affected magazines in the past decade is the rapid growth of digital circulation. In some respects, this can seem a little odd when compared with other media. The World Wide Web was, after all, invented in 1989 and even if it did not begin to gain widespread usage until the late 1990s the effects of the internet on other media – most notably newspapers and music – were felt much earlier.

And yet, until the second decade of the twenty-first century, it is probably fair to say that magazine brands were still defined as print. Some of this was due to caution (or, at worst, wilful blindness) on the part of publishers: the look and feel of print magazines, to both readers and advertisers, far surpassed anything available in digital format. More significantly, until very recently it was difficult for publishers to make money from their online ventures: advertising revenues were small and readers have proved generally unwilling to pay for most content via a medium where, as the saying goes, 'information wants to be free'.

And yet this only paints a partial picture, even before the massive transformation that has gathered pace since 2010. Digital technologies were changing the nature of print, with magazines having moved to desktop production and then digital printing processes by the 2000s. In some respects, the web was seen as representing just another step in the workflow for a production company, an additional means to generate readers by repurposing content that had settled in stable patterns. Unfortunately for such companies, online technologies – particularly after the arrival of mobile devices capable of displaying high-quality media – proved to be much more disruptive than they had anticipated.

This disruption is very much in evidence for those brands that have seen circulations fall dramatically in the past half-decade. As such, in this chapter I shall consider how circulation has traditionally worked in the magazine industry before looking in more detail at the impact of new systems of digital distribution, particularly for mobile platforms.

The print model

Before concentrating on the impact of the digital revolution, it is worth considering how print magazines are distributed. While it is tempting to refer to this as the 'old' model, with all the implications that such an approach is now defunct, it should also be borne in mind that millions of magazines are still sold this way today and will continue to do so for a long time yet. We have already seen how one magazine, *Newsweek*, famously went digital only in 2013 yet was relaunched as a print title the following year. Indeed, in that same period over 800 print titles were launched in the USA alone, and while many of these will fail that has always been the case in the magazine industry. Print is dead; long live print.

Until the arrival of the internet and digital television, magazines comprised the pre-eminent medium for reaching niche audiences. The trend in the past couple of decades, particularly with the rise of the B2B sector, has been to target ever more clearly defined target markets. Obviously, there is the occasional launch that goes for a mass market, such as the men's weeklies *Nuts* and *Zoo*, but more generally new titles are aimed at a niche market based on what competing companies are producing or current trends.

The starting point for researching magazine markets in the UK is BRAD, a media directory published by Emap that also includes a range of online services (bradinsight.com). It is primarily aimed at advertisers, in that it includes information on rates for all titles carrying advertising in the UK, but is also incredibly useful for anyone looking to set up a new title or wishing to know more about British media.

Print distribution and circulation

Getting a national magazine into a substantial proportion of the estimated 55,000 retail outlets that sell newspapers and magazines in the UK and Eire is no small task, meaning that magazine circulation directors must deal with complex supply chains to get their brands to readers.

The main ways in which magazines reach their customers are via paid copies, free copies (such as supermarket magazines), controlled circulation (to pre-selected readers, for example members of a professional association) and subscription. The most common way for consumer titles to be sold is via newstrade, whether in a retail outlet such as a newsagent or supermarket or a more unusual venue such as a festival or trade show. These are single-copy sales, and while they are responsible for the vast majority of consumer title sales this is not the case for many B2B magazines – nor, indeed, for the highest circulating magazines not aimed at those working in a specific profession or trade.

In addition to dealing with distributors who arrange deals with wholesalers for storing copies and then shipping these to newsagents, supermarkets and other stores, the circulation director will have to ensure that subscriptions are managed efficiently and look for new potential readers, as well as determine how many copies of a magazine need to be printed. As such, this is one of the most important roles in magazine production and one that works in close association with the publisher.

One immediate effect of ecommerce on sales of print magazines has been the decline of a number of high-street shops. WHSmith, for example, which was the largest outlet for newspapers, books and magazines in the UK, saw sales fall from £1.312 billion in 2010 to £1.178 billion in 2015 (although profits rose from £89 million to £123 million during that same period, mainly through cost cutting and reinvestment in digital operations). For those stores that remain, the other side of the transformation of bricks and mortar sales has been the rise and rise of supermarkets. Tesco owns 3,376 stores compared with 621 for WHSmith (as well as offering its own *Tesco* magazine, one of the largest controlled circulation titles in the UK). Although the number of retail outlets available to magazines has actually increased in the past decade, this disguises a massive growth of supermarkets at the expense of independent retailers – and though individual supermarkets sell more copies, they also stock fewer titles.

There are five layers in the distribution of a print magazine: publisher, distributor, wholesaler, retailer, reader. After a magazine has been printed it is taken by the distributor to a depot (occasionally more than one) and from there sent out to the wholesaler network. While it is possible for a publisher to undertake their own distribution, this is incredibly difficult at a national level in a highly competitive market for all but the largest publishers. Alternatively, specialist titles may engage in 'affinity sales', whereby the magazine is sold in a sympathetic outlet, for example music magazines in music shops.

Publishers will usually work through a magazine distributor, with the main four in the UK being Frontline (jointly owned by Bauer Media, Immediate Media and Haymarket), Seymour (now owned by Frontline now that Dennis Publishing has sold its share), Comag (jointly owned by Hearst Magazines and Condé Nast) and Marketforce (TimeInc.). These companies act as intermediaries between printers and wholesale distributors, typically Smith News (part of WHSmith) and Menzies Distribution, who complete the supply chain to retail stores.

Sometimes the same distributor will also be responsible for sending out subscription copies to readers. Alternatively, publishers can use what is known as a 'fulfilment bureau' to handle subscriptions or deal with these in-house. One service available to distributors and publishers is Presstream, a Royal Mail service that offers discounts for publications that exceed volumes of 1,000 per mailing and contain a minimum of one-sixth editorial content. More information on Presstream can be found at royalmail.com.

Magazine circulations

Thus far in this chapter I have considered the processes by which printed magazines are distributed to their readers. Without copies sold in newsagents and supermarkets or delivered via subscription, there would be nothing to read. Except that, as has been noted many times previously, there are fewer readers than before, as can be seen from comparing the best-selling magazine titles from 2007 and 2015 (see Tables 3.1 and 3.2).

The bare statistics are dramatic. In 2007, the top ten bestselling titles in the UK accounted for nearly 9.5 million copies between them each month; in 2015, that number is just below 6 million, a decline of more than a third. In the earlier period, there were five titles with circulations above 1 million – now there are just two, and these depend on older readers for their high sales.

The biggest cause of this decline is, of course, the rise of digital distribution (and, indeed, the figures for 2015 *include* digital copies for these titles, which they did not in 2007). The prospects are not entirely bleak, however. Dennis Publishing's *The Week*, for example, now sells more copies than when it was launched 20 years ago, while *Foodism*, originally set up as a web site, entered the print magazine top 100 in 2015 with more than 100,000 copies distributed. The focus for many titles, however, is increasingly digital – hoping, no doubt, to follow the success of *The Economist*, electronic sales of which grew 226 per cent over a year in the UK to hit more than 70,000 copies. Overall, the news weekly now sells more than 282,000 digital copies worldwide; this is still considerably smaller than print, at 1.26 million worldwide, but the growth of the latter is extremely modest by comparison.

Michael Brunt, *The Economist*'s Managing Director of circulation, observed that he had witnessed a steady migration to digital and that while most subscribers currently prefer the print *and* digital option at the moment, it is in the numbers for digital only that the real change took place in 2015.

For a magazine such as *The Economist*, the benefits of digital are immensely clear: not only can it provide greater convenience for readers but, in addition, digital distribution is considerably cheaper for publishers, cutting out the supply chain outlined earlier in this chapter. As Brunt remarked of the 2015

Table 3.1 UK top ten paid titles, July 2007

Title	Average circulation per issue
What's On TV	1,437,650
TV Choice	1,353,436
Northern and Shell women's weeklies	1,350,801
Radio Times	1,082,338
Take a Break	1,027,013
Reader's Digest	717,285
BBC pre-school magazines	654,880
Closer	614,141
Heat	598,623
Saga Magazine	610,771

Table 3.2 UK top ten paid titles, July 2015

Title	Average circulation per issue
TV Choice	1,276,045
What's on TV	1,013,702
Radio Times	712,927
Take a Break	608,743
Slimming World	539,437
Saga Magazine	400,647
Good Housekeeping	385,638
Glamour	366,068
Woman & Home	326,417
Closer	281,136

circulation figures: 'We've enjoyed the benefits of this trend for some time and it's a great position to be in.' For certain brands that are respected and valued highly by their readers the digital revolution is an even better way to reach new readers – and one that can be much more profitable than the print model ever was.

The rise of digital magazines

As shown in the brief history of magazines in Chapter 1, digital magazines are not new *per se*, having been around since the mid-1990s. What has changed is the impact and significance of digital magazines, which for many readers are now the primary way to engage with a brand. Such titles were often referred to as ezines in prior decades, partly from the vogue of inserting 'e' before everything digital to demonstrate its novelty, but also in some cases to demonstrate the inferiority of such products: they were not *proper* magazines but a junior and, at best, amusing offshoot.

Clearly that is no longer the case. Digital magazines now have their own awards (digitalmagazineawards.com), sponsored by publishing agencies such as Edition Digital, the *Guardian* and Magvault. Finalists in the 2015 competition such as *Computer Arts*, *Metal Hammer* and the winner, *Wired*, have taken to digital media, particularly mobile, with aplomb, showing creativity and inventiveness. While *The Economist* probably deserves the crown as the leading digital publication in the UK at the moment, *Wired* in particular shows just what can be done in a digital environment.

Although, as already noted in the Introduction, print remains the core business for most publishers, for a significant minority the future will be mostly – if not entirely – digital. Since the mid-2000s, there have been plenty of smaller titles that have launched as a web-only title, taking advantage of the cheaper distribution costs of the internet but some such as *London Fashion News* (londonfashionnews.com) and *TechRadar* (techradar.com) have become leading influencers in their fields and can be substantial operations.

Figure 3.1 The Digital Magazine Awards web site

Added to this, some titles that were once print have now moved completely online, whether distributed through their own web sites or via a content store such as those for Apple or Google. Brands such as *Design Week* (designweek. co.uk) and the *Journalist* (nuj.org.uk/about/the-journalist-magazine/) started life in print but now can reach their professional audiences more easily through the web. This is largely a feature of B2B brands; for consumer titles, it is more likely to represent a commercial failure to go digital only.

One unfortunate example of this was *Company* magazine. Owned by Hearst and first published in 1978, it promoted a lifestyle brand aimed at younger women than its sister title, *Cosmopolitan*. Once one of Hearst's most popular titles with a circulation above half a million at the start of the millennium, by the time its last print edition was published in 2014 that figure had dropped to less than 90,000. It had built up a strong online presence, especially on social media sites such as Facebook, Twitter and Instagram, and Hearst announced that the title would go digital only. While an offshoot, *Company High Street Edit*, is still available via app stores, activity on its various social media outlets has been moribund since the summer of 2015, with the web site being rolled up into that for *Cosmopolitan*.

Despite the example of *Company* – which faced the challenge of appealing to a demographic (young women between 16 and 24) who are as likely to follow bloggers and home-grown YouTubers as established brands – for many publishers the future does not look quite so bleak. After a decade of denial, panic and existential despair, many are beginning to find ways to make money from their digital offerings. Kristen Nicole Holderman (2013) has observed, the magazine without a web site is a rare animal today and that 'as digital technologies advance, so do its users, and so must the content providers'. That means that brands need to be where their readers are – flicking through the pages of a print edition, browsing a web site or, more often than not, using apps on their mobile phone.

Digital strategies and considerations

One noticeable and very welcome change is that – for web sites at least – most publishers have moved beyond treating digital as a dumping ground for content from their print titles. In other formats, there is still work to be done; thus, for example, it isn't hard to find digital editions on a site such as Zinio that are simply PDFs of the print version and unreadable on all but the largest and sharpest of tablets. Considering how much care and attention is paid by publishers to the look and appearance of their print products, transferring these to an entirely unsuitable medium makes it unsurprising that consumers are unwilling to exchange money for these titles.

Leaving the particular challenges of mobile aside for one moment, it is worth considering some of the special requirements raised by the web as a means of distribution, of which three – finding content, multimedia and generating revenue – stand out.

I have looked at some of the features of generating revenue in the previous chapter but, bearing in mind Mark Twain's pithy observation that 'the lack of money is the root of all evil', it is also worth noting the potential use of paywalls in addition to more familiar models such as advertising and subscription. A paywall, where readers cannot access web content without a paid sub-scription, has been more common in the newspaper industry than for magazine brands although a few titles have experimented with them, such as *Esquire* and *The Atlantic*.

It is worth noting that 'hard' paywalls – where no information is available without a subscription (as is found on *The Times, Financial Times* or *The Wall Street Journal* for example) – are rare for magazines. Indeed, *The Wall Street Journal's WSJ Magazine* is freely available as the one part of its web site open to the public. More common is the model of a 'soft' or metered paywall, where some access is allowed, usually a limited number of articles to be read before

Figure 3.2 WSJ Magazine

subscription is required. This is the model used by *The Economist* and is one reason for its very successful digital strategy.

Peter Marsh, who undertook research into newspaper paywalls in 2014 observed that retention rates for metered rates are much higher than for hard pay-walls, with publishers of the latter often reporting retention rates as low as 15–20 per cent, compared with an average of 58.5 per cent for metered sites and as high as 90 per cent.

The appeal of magazine brands, however, is that after a decade of experiment-ing with bloggers and Google Adwords advertisers are once more recognising the advantages of being associated with a respected publisher. As Guy Consterdine (2005: 6) observes: 'the intimacy between reader and magazine benefits advertisers . . . In the sympathetic context of the right magazine, the strong positive brand values of the magazine can transfer onto the advertisers.' Though Consterdine was mainly writing about print, the same holds true for digital environments.

With regard to finding articles on the web, if, according to the well-worn phrase, content is king then search-engine optimisation (SEO) is queen. I shall focus more on the specifics of producing SEO-friendly content in the next chapter, but a few standards are worth bearing in mind. Larry Page, co-founder of Google, once said that the perfect search engine 'understands exactly what you mean and gives you back exactly what you want'. Meanwhile, back in the real world, journalists and publishers need to craft their content to take advantage of search engines such as Google and Bing.

One element is not to overestimate the intelligence of machines which, while far superior to humans in the speed of many of their calculations, are no match for some of the most basic features of communication (such as puns) which humans can master while still children. As such, clarity matters, as does creat-ing content that earns links from other sites; in an age of shovelware, quality matters.

Structure is important, meaning that intros should be well written and there should be clear headings. Likewise, any multimedia content (audio, video, photos) should be tagged so that terms readers are likely to enter into a search engine will show up. But this is the most important final point: in the end, your users are readers, not search engines.

Multimedia has been one of the most exciting – and initially terrifying – aspects of digital production for publishers. Plenty of brands now run their own YouTube or Vimeo channels where they produce rather than just host videos for others; in some respects, this is no more than an extension of the multimedia revolution that took over magazines in the late nineteenth and early twentieth centuries as publishers began to appeal to readers with illustrations and then photography. Indeed, without even entering the specialist world of audio and video, one of the best web sites for photography – nationalgeographic.com – brings the spectacular power of the image to the web just as it did for print.

And yet, as Jim Gaines, then editor of TimeInc., observed in 2009, publishers were slow to take advantage of the full virtues of what was available through digital media:

> If you're interested in yachting, why would you confine yourself to words on paper and still images? You'd want to see races . . . to see people building boats and hear great America's Cup captains talk about racing. There are so many ways to experience a subject that aren't ink on paper.
> Glaser 2009

The power of mobile

One of the most important changes to have taken place for the magazine market since the publication of the first edition of *Magazine Production* is the development of mobile platforms capable of delivering content to readers in a format that they want to consume.

Mobile phones and tablets existed before Apple began to sell the iPhone in 2007 and the iPad in 2010, but the ways in which these two devices revolutionised mobile platforms cannot be underestimated. Before the first iPhone (which did not include support for apps), nearly every mobile phone available to users consisted of a small screen and a keyboard, with interfaces that were frequently difficult to use. By turning as much of the surface of the phone into a touch screen – one that by the release of the iPhone 4 had a high-resolution, or 'retina', display – Apple provided a large enough area for publishers to be finally tempted to consider releasing content aimed specifically at mobile phones. This in turn was helped by the launch of the App Store a year later, allowing users to download software specifically designed for their phones rather than having to rely on fiddly web sites intended for much larger computer displays.

For magazines, the iPad was a much more important development in many respects. With a screen dimension of nearly 10 inches, it more closely approximated the format of print titles (which, unfortunately, had one side effect of prompting too many publishers simply to release unoptimised PDFs of their print titles). Tablets were not invented by Apple: Microsoft had worked on a tablet-based specification in the 1990s, but the devices produced were too bulky, power-hungry and expensive for consumers. In addition, the Windows operating system was far too complex to use without a stylus or input devices such as mouse and keyboard and the concept didn't take off before 2010.

With Google's Android entering as a competitor to Apple iOS in 2008, followed by the somewhat poorly received Windows 8 in 2012, the mobile market for both smartphones and tablets has grown massively in the past decade, with the number of smartphone users estimated to pass two billion in 2016 and tablet users approximately half that number. This bald statistic covers a number of complexities; for example, that the tablet market seems to be declining as many users turn to larger phones as their primary or sole device and, in any case, do not upgrade tablets anywhere near as much as phones.

Nonetheless, the important point is that mobile technology has now saturated users' perceptions, often providing the main means by which they engage with media across a wide variety of formats. For magazine brands, it is important to pay attention to the platforms and ecosystems available to mobile users, as well as the apps they may use, and to think of design specifically for smaller devices.

Apple itself heralded the iPad as a device that would be especially helpful to publishers, as indicated by its launch of Newsstand with iOS 5 in 2012. This was intended to woo publishers to the iPad in tandem with iTunes, and doubtlessly Apple hoped to do for the publishing industry what it had for music with the original iPod and iTunes earlier in the century.

There were a number of problems with Apple's approach, however. First of all, Apple took 30 per cent of subscriptions but this loss of revenue in many respects was less important than the strict terms imposed on publishers, reducing their options to cut deals with existing subscribers (a common tactic to promote sales, whereby publishers take a loss in the first year which is then recouped with renewals). Apple also severed the relations between publishers and readers, allowing neither direct marketing nor the collection of information that is incredibly valuable to brands looking to build closer relations. Finally, the publishing industry was not in quite the same dire situation as music had been after the emergence of peer-to-peer file sharing at the turn of the millennium.

As such, publishers were at best lukewarm towards Newsstand and Apple seemed to lose interest in the project. As Glenn Fleishman (2014) remarked, 'after some fanfare, and major publications adopting the Newsstand format . . . Apple more or less left it to rot'.

Nonetheless, while Newsstand was ultimately a failure (being removed from iOS 9), apps were here to stay and quickly became the favourite way for users to interact with their mobile devices. As well as being devised for phones or tablets – with an emphasis on simplicity of usability that suited a touch interface rather than mouse and keyboard, and often cleaner designs than corresponding web pages – apps had another important impact. In contrast to the

Figure 3.3 The Apple Newsstand app

open standards of the web, an app developed for iOS wouldn't work on Android nor, before Windows 10, would it work on Microsoft's platform. Add to this Amazon's forking of the original Android specification for its Fire tablets and other bit players such as (briefly) BlackBerry and HP WebOS, and it was clear that the technology market was likely to fragment in a way that had not been seen since the 1990s, as each platform sought to build its own ecosystem of apps and content.

In practice, a degree of sanity and maturation has returned to the market, in part helped out by the fact that two operating systems – iOS and Android – dominate phones, each accounting for 13.9 per cent and 82.8 per cent respectively. That means that most users will be looking to either the Apple App Store or Google Play to purchase apps and content.

At nearly seven times the number of users as iOS, it would seem obvious to publishers that they should develop for Android first, but the truth is often the other way around. Because they are more expensive than Android phones, iPhone users tend to be more affluent which means that they also tend to spend more on content as well as the devices themselves (in 2013, according to research conducted by the International Data Corporation, iPhone owners were twice as likely to be in the $100,000 income category as Android owners, and nearly twice as likely to engage in mcommerce, that is ecommerce via their mobile devices).

A report by App Annie (appannie.com) for the third quarter of 2015 showed that while app downloads from Google Play was 90 per cent higher than on the iOS App Store, when it came to revenue the situation was reversed, with Apple bringing in 80 per cent more in sales than Google. The difference is driven because of the widespread adoption of Android in emerging markets such as India, Indonesia and Vietnam, where sub-$50 phones are bringing ever larger numbers of people online. At the same time, the iPhone 6 and 6 Plus – Apple's first foray into larger format phones – were immensely popular in China which, along with the USA and Europe, has become the focus for Apple sales.

As such, developers and producers tend to devise products for iOS first as there is a greater chance of recouping costs, but in truth the Android market is so huge that only the very foolish would ignore it. Publishers need to be where their readers are and, increasingly, that means on their phones.

Social media

Along with the more mature technology of the web and the more recent emergence of smartphones, a technological development that has profound implications for magazine publishers is social media.

In some respects, social media is nearly as old as the internet itself, having first emerged in the form of bulletin board systems (BBSes) in the 1970s, where users could leave text messages for each other. But while these were esoteric systems, often complex to use and, in any case, only known to the smallest fraction of the population, contemporary sites such as Facebook, YouTube and Twitter now measure their users in the hundreds of millions and dominate the top ten web sites for traffic alongside search engines such as Google, Yahoo and Baidu. The ease with which they allow users to connect to each other and share video, images and audio is one reason for their popularity, and a far cry from the slow, modem-driven text systems of those early BBSes.

Social media sites are especially important to publishers because, although free to users in terms of financial cost, they generate huge amounts of data about visitors' activities and interests. Effectively, these are the largest databases of human likes and dislikes ever created, something that has often been attempted in other media in an attempt to discern what will appeal to an audience but never on a scale such as evidenced by Facebook, Google and Amazon.

Indeed, along with Apple, these companies have completely transformed the media landscape and are often referred to as the 'Big Four' (sometimes the Big Five with the inclusion of Microsoft). In terms of distribution, if not production, they have changed users' viewing and reading habits to a vast extent – and the fact that three of them barely existed at the turn of the millennium, when the post-war media industry was dominated by companies such as Time Warner, Sony and BMG that had been in existence for most of the twentieth century in one form or another, is testimony to just how seismic the change has been.

The big media companies that had mastered twentieth-century technologies such as broadcasting and mass printing were ill-equipped to deal with the implications wrought by computers and the internet, as indicated by the fact that, for the first decade of the twenty-first century, many of them spent more time attempting to shore up their old, revenue-generating products instead of actively seeking ways to engage with the new digital economy. First the web and then mobile proved extremely disruptive for their ways of doing business, particularly as the barriers between production and consumption became blurred by the user-generated content on which the new breed of companies increasingly came to depend.

Much of the twentieth-century technology that had enabled mass media to exist – large-scale printing or the ability to broadcast first radio and then television – had been expensive to create and distribute. By contrast, the world is now filled with vast numbers of people with recording equipment that was completely inconceivable 20 years ago. At its worst, this means a lot of cat videos (which I like as much as the next man) and baby clips (not so much), but at its best it has also meant a revolution in our understanding of the world, one where we increasingly rely on citizen journalists to discover what is taking place in places as diverse as Syria or Ferguson, Missouri.

Traditional magazine brands, like all other forms of traditional media, do not have the same control over social media platforms such as Twitter, Facebook and Instagram, but many have quickly realised that a fully fledged digital strategy must take into account such sites. In particular, social media allows brands to engage with their readers, building communities as well as content through conversation.

Such conversation is important: when brands treat social media as no more than a cheap marketing tool to drive consumers to their web sites things can quickly go wrong, particularly when faced with an audience that has the ability to express itself en masse as never before. One such social media gaffe occurred when the US company DiGiorno Pizza appropriated the hashtag #WhyIStayed to promote its pizza deliveries, apparently unaware that the tag was trending because of its use as part of an anti-domestic abuse campaign in the aftermath of video footage that showed a footballer attacking his wife.

360° media

In contrast to the kind of mistakes made by DiGiorno Pizza, magazines are usually more sure-footed when dealing with their audiences, in some cases having almost a century's experience of dealing with mass participation in some form or another. The most popular brands such as *Time*, *National Geographic* and *The Economist*, for example, have in excess of ten million followers on Twitter and use platforms such as this to engage in conversation with their followers, to comment on a more informal basis on events that will appeal to them and to provide some leadership in shaping how the public may perceive those events.

For smaller titles, social media can also be an incredibly valuable tool for finding like-minded enthusiasts, as well as fulfilling the vital task of referring visitors to the magazine or web site. For special interest brands, it was always much harder to reach those enthusiasts through traditional means such as direct mailing because of the costs involved, and social media has been utterly transformative in providing new ways to connect with their audiences.

The Magazine Publishers' Association (MPA, magazine.org) releases a quarterly 'Magazine Media 360°' report to track the performance of magazine brands beyond the printed page, looking in particular at the audiences for 166 magazines across Facebook, Twitter, Google+, Instagram and Pinterest. At its simplest, 360° media (a term which was first used more widely by broadcasters than print publishers) means engaging with your audience wherever they may be, and as the story of media consumption in the twenty-first century is one of fragmentation compared with the mass platforms of the twentieth, this means a willingness to participate across as many platforms as possible.

By the final quarter of 2015, the MPA recorded that Facebook comprised about half of the measured magazines' entire social media audience, with a total of 389 million followers. Twitter followed with an audience of 162 million, then Google+ with 133 million, Instagram with 91 million and Pinterest with 24 million. While the audience for magazines on Facebook grew around 6 per cent, Instagram showed the biggest increase, expanding 30.1 per cent in the last three months of 2015.

Figure 3.4 MPA's Magazine Media 360° social media report

When broken down by single titles, *National Geographic* boasts the largest social media following across various platforms, with more than 90 million accounts registered as followers. Next comes *ESPN, The Magazine*, with 47 million followers, then *Time* (26.4 million), *The Economist* (26.3 million) and *Vogue* (24.9 million). *National Geographic* is in the top three social media platforms, with the exception of Pinterest, and is also the fastest growing magazine brand on social media, having almost doubled its presence in a year.

The potential for engagement with an audience is staggering. *National Geographic* has a worldwide circulation of 6.7 million, an extremely respectable figure even if the number has declined by some 100,000 since 2013. Those figures, however, pale next to the brand's digital presence. As well as its 90 million social media followers, 26 million people visit its web site each month, while millions more download apps to mobile devices to view photographs and articles. It is not without reason that the company talks of a 'brand universe'.

Of course, the sceptically minded could argue that it is those 6.7 million purchasers of the magazine subscriptions (currently $34 a year, though frequently discounted below that) who really matter, but ignoring even the potential advertising base for the web site, *National Geographic*'s brand universe demonstrates a remarkable ability to reach out to readers, far greater than could ever have been achieved by print alone.

Conversation and communities

Specialist magazines have long seen themselves as creating communities. In the 1990s, Paul Theberge (1997) examined how music titles worked to build up bodies of readers as active participants in the scene over the preceding two decades, and for a century or more readers' letters pages had served as a basic forum for interaction.

Social media has made feedback and engagement with readers much more immediate, and the MPA media report contains some fascinating insights into what that audience really cares about. On Facebook, for example, motorcycle and automative articles are most likely to be shared, as well as those dealing with green issues, fishing and hunting and the Hispanic community. For Twitter users, articles on luxury items and spectator sports are more important, while Instagram's community shares images dealing with travel, fashion and, unsurprisingly, photography. These communities also demonstrate the changing nature of user engagement, whereby participants move from being readers, to listeners as podcasts caught on, to watchers as more and more brands use video, to content creators themselves, sharing their own creations via content hubs. The immediacy with which social media operates means that timely engagement with readers is even more important, which is why a social media strategy is increasingly crucial.

The hope for any brand, of course, is that an article goes viral, spreading through the magazine's audience and beyond with a mysterious life of its own. There is no magic formula for creating viral content, despite the many silicon snake-oil web sites promising instant success, but it is important that the important details that editors and journalists have concentrated on for a long time are still adhered to. A story should obviously be appealing to most of the audience and worth sharing with friends and family. For any chance of it being spread, of course it needs to be on a platform such as Facebook or Twitter that allows easy sharing, and the ability to write tight and compelling headlines is as important as ever. It goes without saying that the content should be of good quality: clickbait (which, in the end, is what the more disreputable viral marketers offer) provides short-term success at best. If you mislead your readers with a false title and then fail to deliver, they are unlikely to trust you again.

The issue of quality cannot be understated, and will be dealt with more in the following chapter when I turn to editorial. It is worth making a final point about the digital revolution that has taken place in magazine publishing over the past decade. The ability to track visitors to a web site, or downloads to mobile devices, has led publishers to become more obsessed than ever with analysing statistics. Alexis Madrigal (2012) has drawn attention to what he calls the 'dark social', the sharing of sites via bookmarks, email and instant messaging, a means of communication between audiences that is harder (if not impossible) to track. As with the other universe that surrounds us, much of the activity that takes place in a brand universe is ultimately unseen.

4
Copy and editorial

So far I have looked at the business and context of brands. Now it is time to turn to the actual production of a magazine, beginning with its written content. Subsequent chapters will consider the role of art and design in the production process. Here I shall focus on the typical structure of an editorial department, as well as some of the essential elements for creating good content based around preparation, commissioning and checking/subbing material. Some other features, particularly with regard to ethical and legal factors that have to be considered by editors, are considered in Chapter 7.

The role of the editor

Journalistic skills and management are key to the role of the editor. While he or she has to engage with every level of production throughout the magazine, it is also important that the editor has the maturity to take legal and moral responsibility for everything that appears in the title and can delegate the necessary tasks to ensure that it is published on deadline. In addition to working within the title, the editor is also the main representative, alongside the publisher, of the brand to the outside world; for readers in particular, he or she will often be the person most associated with the brand, and so will have to provide leadership to his or her team to shape its purpose and mission.

Ideally, the editor will have worked in just about every aspect of journalism, whether editorial work for news, features and reviews or as a sub-editor. In practice, he or she will only have fulfilled a few of these aspects, but still the editor needs to understand how each area of their title functions and how to bring them together into a complete package.

On smaller titles, with very small editorial teams, the editor may also be a *de facto* contributor to each and every section, while on larger publications he or she may delegate responsibilities to section editors. Nonetheless, it is still important for the editor to be able to write copy, sub-edit and draft headlines or captions; with this comes confidence but also an understanding of how these different elements work.

Routes into editing

The two routes into editing tend to involve those who come from a writing background and those who come from production. The journalistic requirements for a reporter or feature writer can be very different to those of a sub-editor: a writer will need to substantiate the facts of their story and collate together all their sources, engaging in research to produce the best copy that they can write.

A sub, on the other hand, is more concerned with clarity and consistency, and very often that content 'fits' with other parts of the magazine and deadlines. In addition, subs, working closely with a design department, have to pay attention to those elements that make a title or article stand out – the eye-grabbing headline or well-placed picture, cover lines and standfirsts that will make a reader on the newsstand pick up the magazine in the first place.

The skills that come from production are immensely useful to an editor in that they enable him or her to see the shape of the brand, how word counts are transformed into columns and pages that, in turn, become sections and finally the whole product combining editorial and advertising in a format that is most appealing to an audience. In addition, working closely with a production department will provide an editor with a clearer understanding of the technicalities of design, printing and distribution as well as online cycles. He or she will know what can or cannot work – the nuts and bolts of which will be left to the subs and production editors.

Those editors who come from a writing background, however, will also have other, extremely important abilities. Being an editor means that you are not – should not – be bound to the desk; success in this area comes from speaking to people, and reporters and writers will have to interview subjects on a daily basis, building up contacts, working with PR agencies, dealing with clients and strangers. The editor has to be willing to speak to anyone (or have very good reasons not to), as he or she is the public face of the story.

Likewise, while a good sub will recognise those visual and verbal clues that appeal to readers, a reporter has the nose for a good story and needs constantly to come up with new ideas. When he or she has the skill to turn this into a compelling narrative, this is something that can be taken to another level by the editor who needs to craft a similar narrative for each issue of the magazine, or even the brand itself.

The best editors will combine elements of both writing and production: the demands of a deadline or a particular layout should not be allowed to dilute or distort the impact of a good writer's work – in the worst of cases the need to make a story fit a column could end up with erroneous statements that are potentially libellous. At the same time, a talented freelance may not have the reader fully in mind.

Editing and management

Beyond these writing and technical skills, it should never be forgotten that editing is also a managerial role – something that can often hinder those who have worked their way up the ranks and developed an 'us and them' mentality with regard to the management. The level of management given to an editor will vary from title to title, but it will nearly always involve some level of budget control, such as freelance payments and expenses, legal decisions with regard to what will appear in the magazine, people skills to ensure that a team pulls together to produce the magazine, and usually responsibility for hiring and firing staff.

As well as being the main figurehead who bridges the brand's staff and readers, an editor has an important part to play within a magazine as the bridge between editorial and other departments. While magazine editors often wish to stand apart from the business of publishing, this is unlikely to be a successful strategy in today's commercial market.

Editors and publishers

The editor must be willing to engage with the publisher, marketing departments and (often the most tricky) the media sales team. While a good editor will have a vision of where the brand is going – and must be willing to stand up for it against the demands of a publisher and advertisers if he or she sees that they will affect readers of the magazine adversely – ultimately the best brands are those in which all aspects of magazine publishing and production work in some sort of harmony.

As publishers often come from a sales background, there can be a sense of disdain towards editorial staff who are seen as somehow 'protected' from the harsh economic realities of magazine sales. (In practice, editors may also prefer a degree of this disdain – publishers who come from editorial may be a much worse burden in terms of their levels of interference.)

Editors who neglect commercial concerns are liable to drag their title into financial difficulties – for example, by alienating too many advertisers or readers; at the same time, an editor who is concerned only with profit above all things is unlikely to produce a magazine that can be trusted by the general public. The editor must always be willing to stand up for the interests of his or her staff, to ensure that the pages they create and which, ultimately, sell the magazine, can follow the route that will always take into account what attracts readers to the title in the first place.

This brings us to the final role of the editor, as an advocate for the reader. He or she should provide leadership, both internally to members of an editorial team, and also externally in terms of having something to say rather than simply following fashions. At the same time, an editor who neglects his or her readership to follow personal hobby horses could soon be presiding over a rapidly declining circulation.

There is a danger in all this of becoming too oriented towards a 'focus-group' mentality, in which no editorial decision is made without consulting readers in some way: an experienced editor will often have good hunches about what the public wants, rather than what it thinks it wants. Nonetheless, the writer (and it is usually editors coming from a writing background who display this tendency) who thinks only of what he or she wants to say without regard for the consequences is probably far too arrogant to lead a magazine.

Editorial and production

The editor, as outlined above, will have responsibility for two main areas of the magazine, namely editorial (writing) and production, incorporating subbing and design. If there is no substantial design work to be done, and a title does not appear too frequently, it is not uncommon for an editor to commission a layout artist to produce a template for a magazine which he or she can complete for each issue.

It is much more common, however, for magazines to work with an in-house team comprising several members of staff. At the smallest, these may be specialist newsletters comprising one or two writers with design being handled by a centralised production department, with slightly larger titles consisting of an editor and editorial assistant, plus an art editor and sub-editor (both of whom may be full- or part-time). For such publications, commissioning is handled by the editor and most of the actual content is likely to be produced by freelances, with the assistant ensuring that administrative tasks such as dealing with invoices and taking calls are dealt with.

Section editors

For regular monthly magazines with substantial pagination, a dedicated, larger editorial team becomes a necessity – not least because there must be sufficient staff to cover holidays. While the editor provides overall leadership and is responsible for planning the flow of copy, much of the day-to-day administration will be delegated to a deputy editor and/or section editors.

Who these editors are will vary according to the make-up of the magazine; for example, a news editor if news stories are important, a features editor or number of features editors covering different aspects of a magazine's make-up. Such staff will be responsible for commissioning content for each issue and will generally be in more constant contact with freelances. In addition, they will be delegated work from the editor that involves going out and speaking to people about the magazine; a music reviews editor, for example, will need to attend events that involve the music industry.

Working under these editors will be reporters and staff writers whose respons- ibilities are more generally limited to producing copy, although as they tend to be assigned a 'beat' – a topic to keep abreast of – such writers will be expected to maintain a list of contacts, attend press conferences where necessary and interview subjects for their articles.

For a medium- to large-sized magazine, the production department will usually consist of some form of managing or production editor alongside an art depart- ment. The production editor (considered in more detail in Chapter 5) has the important job of ensuring that the trains run on time; once a schedule is agreed for production, he or she will need to liaise with departments to make sure that, for example, copy comes in when required and that it is subbed and returned to editors for a final check. As he or she often has control of the flat-plan, another important task will be liaising with the advertising director: changes to the number of advertising pages coming in can have important consequences for how editorial is arranged.

While the production editor is usually in charge of sub-editors, alongside these there will often be an art department. The art editor has the main responsibility for the look and feel of a magazine, in conjunction with the editor, and will often be the manager of a team of graphic artists whose job it is to lay out pages and possibly produce graphics. In addition, he or she will commission illustr- ations and photography. For multi-title companies, both elements of produc- tion (subbing and design) are often centralised, with teams working across several magazines.

Although not part of the in-house team, a final important constituent for most titles is its stable of freelances. Any editor will seek to build up a collection of reliable writers, designers and photographers that he or she can call on to provide content for different issues. The virtue of using freelances is flexibility: if budgets are tight, content can be cut back and then increased if the demand grows. The disadvantages can include less control over work (which is why the issue of reliability becomes so important), and potential difficulties regarding rights over content.

Editorial planning

The editorial process can be incredibly complex for magazines with large teams and substantial numbers of contributors, and it is the task of the production editor and editor to work out a schedule that can bring together all elements of a title into a finished product. Copy and graphics must be sourced, content checked for quality and accuracy, laid out and subbed in accordance with a house style, and the whole lot checked again before being despatched to a printer.

This is not a linear procedure, in that different people will be working on different parts of the magazine at the same time and passing content back and forth between them. Keeping track of this is much easier if there is a system in place to plan ahead.

The lead-in time for a monthly magazine, from the moment when articles are commissioned to when they appear in print, is typically around six weeks. The full process of creating a schedule will be discussed in Chapter 5 when dealing with the role of the production editor; here I will concentrate on the task of planning for editorial.

For a web site, the schedule will be very different and is closer to that for a newspaper in some respects, particularly if the brand is a B2B title that also wishes to keep its readers abreast of news. In such instances, the production team will be dealing with a content-management system of some form and, as we shall see in Chapter 6, this will require more regular updates.

The editorial calendar

Before commissioning can take place, the editor and his or her team require a calendar, which will usually consist of several forms. Any title working in a particular market will have a set of annual events which are more or less fixed from year to year. For a fashion magazine, it will be the launch of new collections, for an automobile title there will be the big trade shows and registration changeovers. There are things throughout the year that readers will expect to be covered, and seasonal changes from summer to winter will affect what people are buying and looking for.

Onto these bare bones, an editor will then try to second-guess what will be significant in the market for the coming year. A 12-month calendar will only be sketchy, but when planning ahead for six months and three months, this will start to include more and more detail.

While long-term editorial planning is, to some degree, always a little futile in that fashions change, it is an attempt to make the unpredictable a little more routine and is also essential not merely for working out what contributions will be made by journalists and designers, but also for sales and marketing teams: if they have an idea of what will be appearing in the magazine three issues down the line, they can begin to contact potential advertisers and plan press releases.

By the time a three-month calendar is drawn up, planning for an issue will become much more serious. At the stage when one issue is being completed, commissioning editors will be thinking of who to approach not simply for the next magazine, but the one after that. The process of editorial planning will run more or less along the following lines:

- The first step will be a planning meeting of some sort with section editors, where ideas are discussed and names put forward. In addition, a tentative running order and estimate of pagination will be outlined. Increasingly, production editors may have two calendars – one for print and another for online.
- Commissioning editors locate suitable writers, photographers and so on and find out whether they will be willing to take on work. If so, a detailed brief is drawn up, alongside some form of letter of contract indicating terms and conditions (although, with regular contributors, this will probably be no more than an email indicating the price for the work). In-house writers will also be briefed on what they need to produce for the forthcoming issue.
- The production editor will draw up a flat-plan, a 'map' of the magazine that becomes extremely important for organising the workflow of the issue. They may also be responsible for managing the daily process of uploading material to a web site.
- When copy comes in, the copy-editing process begins: this used to involve filing away typescripts, but these days submissions will be in digital format – not simply for the convenience of delivery via email, but also because it is easier to strip out text from a word-processed document and lay it out in a DTP application such as Adobe InDesign.
- A commissioning editor will read through the article and ensure that it fulfils the brief; if not, it is sent back to the writer or passed along to

someone in-house to rewrite. This is one reason why deadlines for submission must be early enough to allow time to adjust text – although if this is a common occurrence then the editor must consider if he or she is clear enough when writing a brief, or whether it would be better to find new contributors. Sometimes, however, a rewrite is simply necessary: a freelance may follow a brief to the letter, but circumstances change and a story needs to be recast.

- When final copy is accepted, it is then passed to subs who read through looking for obvious errors and ensure that it is in accordance with the house style.

- The next stage is for copy to be laid out by designers, which will be covered in more detail in the next chapter.

- After layout, copy is returned to subs for rechecking – an important part of the process; when a designer is working on a page, his or her main concern is to make it look as good as possible rather than read accurately. This is very often one of the stages where errors can creep in.

- Once a feature has been subbed, it can be checked again by section editors and passed to the editor to be signed off. While some editors, particularly on large titles, may take a more hands-off approach to commissioning and large parts of the production process, it is important that they read through and sign off as much material as possible. Ultimately, if say an article is libellous, they will have responsibility for that material. The difficulty is that this can create a bottleneck in the process, with too much content waiting the final approval of a busy editor.

While this presents the editorial process in a fairly linear manner, it is important to reiterate that an ongoing title will stagger different parts of the flow of copy. For example, a features editor may start commissioning far in advance of the editor responsible for reviews, while the news editor will not find it to his or her advantage to start commissioning stories six weeks in advance of publication.

What this means is that the system outlined above will overlap with different sections of a magazine – and with different issues. At one part of the day, the production editor may be checking that copy is in for the feature section of the January issue and at another be finalising the subbing for news going into the December title.

Flat-planning

A flat-plan is a map of the magazine, detailing where everything will go from the front cover to the back, and its preparation is an extremely important part of the editorial process. A flat-plan will show where editorial and advertising pages are allocated, and the pagination will often be worked out several months in advance as part of the budgeting process discussed in Chapter 2.

A flat-plan will be arranged into sections, with a minimum of four pages to each section (this being the number of pages that will be produced by one sheet of paper, depending on the printing process, with more common quantities being eight or 16). For the production editor, this is an important factor when planning magazine production: different sections can be sent off to start printing, in some cases before the magazine is completed, so deadlines for such things as copy and layout have to be organised so that both editorial and advertising content comes in at the same time for each part of the magazine.

Advertising and editorial

With regard to advertising, determining where ads appear within the title obviously has an impact on the amount of money paid. This can cause more than a little friction: advertisers generally want their display pages as near the front as possible (if the back and inside covers have already been sold), which is why so many magazines have pages of advertising before you hit any editorial. Unsurprisingly, they prefer their ads to face editorial rather than other advertisements, and will always wish to go on the right-hand page (the spot where the eye naturally falls on opening a magazine).

The temptation on the part of the publisher and sales department to push for as many right-hand pages as possible has to be resisted to some degree: too many ads on this side and readers may believe that the magazine has less editorial content than actually exists, making it bad value for money.

In addition, the presence of double-page editorial spreads allows art designers an opportunity to create something with a little more flair: when devising the flat-plan, the task for the editor, working in conjunction with the production editor and art editor, is to create some variety throughout the magazine, so that editorial does not always appear on single, left-hand pages and so looks very dull.

In American magazines, there is a tendency to put aside a portion in the centre of the magazine for editorial only, with no advertising, although this is less common in British titles. One effect of this is that a series of long features, which can be rather text heavy, is broken up so that the first few pages appear in the centre and the rest of the article is located at the end of the magazine.

In the UK, advertisements usually appear between articles and within them, sometimes creating a few problems as too many ads may disrupt a long feature;

that said, too many one-page articles facing each other can be equally disconcerting, and so the placement of ads may be very useful from a design and editorial point of view in terms of helping to differentiate articles from each other.

While editorial pagination will be determined early on during the planning stage, advertising can be slightly more problematic: obviously, the publisher and advertising director will have a budget which determines the number of pages allocated to ads, but ads are usually sold in single pages or DPSs. If the ratio of advertising to editorial is 40:60 (that is 40 pages of advertising against 60 pages of editorial), selling 42 pages means that there will be two pages less of editorial.

The amount of advertising sold tends to fluctuate throughout the year, and editors will need to establish reasonable limits against which the ratio of editorial pages can expand or decrease. If the allocation for advertising pages cannot be hit for some reason, this may leave an editor with the headache of a few extra pages to fill. When planning for this, editors may commission additional material that is not time-sensitive (and so can be carried across to the next issue), or have on hand 'house ads', advertisements for related magazines, that can be inserted into a blank space.

For this reason, a flat-plan is often an evolving rather than static map of the magazine – but to avoid a nervous breakdown the production editor will want it to remain as fixed as possible during the production cycle. Once it has been determined, copies of it will be distributed to the art department, section editors and advertising sales team.

The post-mortem

While planning would seem logically to conclude with sending a magazine 'to bed'; that is, sending files to a printer or uploading to a web site, another important stage is the post-mortem. This is a meeting after the finished magazine has been received, where the editor and his or her team will consider the issue, discussing elements that worked or did not work so well. The aim of the post-mortem is to capitalise on successes and find out why particular failures may have happened and so prevent them occurring again.

News

While news tends, unsurprisingly, to be associated with newspapers, it has an incredibly important role to play in a wide variety of magazines. While general men's and women's magazines probably do not really carry much news of importance – such things as celebrity events and gossip being dealt with on a more efficient basis by the tabloids, with their daily turnaround – other types of consumer magazines may inform their readers in a way that is not dealt with sufficiently by the daily press. News has become even more important as magazines move online, with a constant stream required for certain brands.

It is in B2B titles, however, that magazine news reporting probably really comes into its own: specialist titles for a particular industry or profession need to keep readers up to date with all that is happening, and this kind of expert information is seen as too rarefied to be dealt with in larger-circulation newspapers.

Hicks *et al.* (2008: 11) provide the most straightforward definition of news as that which is 'factual, new and interesting'. As such, it must provide information that, to readers at least, is unknown and which must also be of interest to them. A story on calls for an amnesty on financial clawback for missed targets for British dentists is unlikely to appeal to the nation as a whole, but is important enough to be a lead in *Dentistry Magazine* as it will affect a significant proportion of the audience.

This specificity is probably what distinguishes most magazine news journalism from newspaper news reporting. Obviously journalists on a daily will have a beat, specific areas that they need to report on such as crime or sport, but there is also the fact that readers browsing through different sections of a newspaper will have no, or very little, connection in terms of occupation, age, socio-economic status and interests.

News for magazine audiences

By contrast, for all but the biggest-circulating consumer titles there will be something that ties a magazine to its audience very closely: for the readers of *Auto Express*, new car launches will be extremely important to just about everyone who opens its pages, while *The Lawyer Magazine* is very clearly aimed at a particular class of professionals. Indeed, for B2B titles it is often very sensible to make certain assumptions about the background of potential readers, for example their level of education and expertise in a field, if the title does not wish to appear to talk down to them.

For a long time, magazines could not expect to beat newspapers on topicality although this has changed to a degree as more move online. What they often have, however, is a level of expertise and knowledge about a particular field that is not matched by more generalist papers.

Scoops are not impossible: sometimes events of a much wider significance can be hidden away from the public gaze but are unearthed by a specialist journalist who has the contacts and knowledge to realise something important is going on. Of course, if a scoop does make it into a magazine before the papers and is relevant to a wider audience, editors of the dailies will soon take it up and start uncovering information that can be published more quickly.

The strength of magazines is that news can then lead into much longer features than are typically available for the newspaper format. As such, B2B titles especially can offer greater analysis and in-depth background to news events by drawing upon their links and sources within a particular industry.

Writing magazine news

With the one (extremely important) proviso noted above about taking into account the particular nature of a magazine audience, many of the facets that go into writing news stories for magazines are very similar to those for other media such as newspapers. A news story should be well crafted and also provide an angle, a point of view that establishes why a story makes sense.

This is not the same as propaganda; distorting facts so that they fit a particular purpose is, unfortunately, all too common in journalism and damages the profession. However, a good reporter always has a sense of why a particular story will be of interest to his readers, which in turn is linked to his or her news sense, the experience of knowing why some topics are appealing.

As mentioned previously, there are plenty of good books that will outline the qualities that comprise a good news story, so here I will concentrate simply on outlining the basics.

The six questions and the news pyramid

If anyone knows anything about journalistic writing, it is probably the six questions that every opening paragraph should aspire to answer: who, what, why, where, how and when. Here is an example taken from the *UK Press Gazette*:

> Magazine publisher Hachette Filipacchi (UK) and chief executive Kevin Hand [WHO] are suing Haymarket Media for libel damages. [WHAT] The legal battle centres around a story in *Media Week* magazine [WHERE] in April, [WHEN] headed 'Hachette faces an uncertain future'. [WHY] They are seeking an injunction banning repetition of the allegations made in the story. [HOW]

The six questions are a checklist, a means of providing relevant information as concisely as possible. The information they provide should appear throughout the story, although sometimes a particular element may not be as relevant: who and what are always essential, but the other questions may vary from piece to piece.

Another long-standing formula is the news pyramid, whereby points in a news story are made in descending order of importance. Thus essential details have to appear in the opening paragraph and additional information can then appear later in the story. The reason for this is twofold: sometimes sub-editors will need to cut a story and do not wish to worry about losing essential information; similarly, readers will often skim the beginnings of news stories to get up to speed, then finish reading once their curiosity is satisfied.

With these questions and the notion of the news pyramid in mind, the intro to a news story needs to grab a reader's attention and make sense to them instantly. It should convey the essential facts of a story and should be short – usual recommendations are between 20 and 30 words.

Facts, claims and objectivity

Objectivity is often a touchstone of journalism, and one which raises considerable difficulties on a philosophical, practical and even political level. The question of whether a journalist can ever be truly objective is beyond the scope of this book, and merely selecting the facts as they appear important to the reporter, without any deliberate distortion of evidence, will often introduce an element of bias into a story.

However, on the practical level, the requirement to distinguish facts from claims is an essential journalistic skill. If reporting what purports to be a fact, this needs to be verified as much as humanly possible, as opposed to reporting what is said in speech or a written report. Thus, for example, the fact that a particular movie cost $200 million to make is relatively easy to check, but if someone interviewed for a story tells the reporter that it is the most expensive movie ever made, that is a claim that needs to be identified as such within the story.

When a claim is being presented, it should be clearly indicated: the source of the information should be given, although if this material comes from a press conference or routine interview those facts do not need to be pointed out. For written sources, however, some additional detail (the title of a report, for example) should be provided.

Running stories, news style and structure

Running stories are extremely important in newspapers, where events in a significant case such as a murder inquiry may only unfold over a period of days or weeks. Repeating essential facts (such as the background of a key player) will become irritating very quickly. Periodicals which appear on a monthly or weekly basis may not suffer from this problem quite as much, but if a title is reporting regularly on a major issue that affects its target audience and which they are likely to remember, running or follow-up stories may omit background detail in subsequent issues.

When dealing with style, it is important to remember that news stories need to be as direct and vivid as possible. If the reader cannot determine the main points of a story in the opening paragraph, he or she is unlikely to read on. As news stories typically deal with events that have already happened, then it is normal for them to be told in the past tense. Occasionally, however, a news story will be told in the present tense to make it more vivid, moving to the past tense as the reporter provides factual details.

> Troopideas.com is not exactly 'MySpace for war fighters,' but it's a Web site that invites frontline troops to post their ideas for improving the combat experience. Engineers and developers then use Web 2.0 techniques such as mashups and wikis to turn those ideas into reality.
> PC World

Common styles to make a story more interesting include 'selling' the story – picking up a particular feature in the piece and telling readers why they need to know this fact – and a narrative style more usually found in fiction, establishing a colourful background to the bare facts of the story. Such elements are particularly important to long-form journalism, those pieces that fall somewhere between traditional articles and a novel; indeed, some of the most important magazine journalism of the twentieth century has found its fullest expression in long-form styles, such as John Hersey's 30,000-word feature 'Hiroshima', which was published by *The New Yorker* in 1946.

The virtue of employing a more literary style is that it can be more dramatic than the rather bald who, what, why, where, how and when formula, but the danger is that it can put off readers, either by selling them a detail that does not interest them, or by failing to provide them with essential information that keeps them reading.

Another common technique is the 'delayed drop', usually indicated by the use of the word 'but', which indicates the tenor of the story is about to change in a vivid fashion. This, in turn, indicates the importance of building the structure of a news story. Where a delayed drop is not used, it is more usual to build the pyramid, retelling the short, punchy intro with more detail. Alternatively, the reporter may build up the story by providing the background events that led to the series of facts given in the first paragraph. As the story progresses, quotes and further supporting evidence can be introduced.

The role of the news editor

While the business of spotting news is something that can be spread throughout an entire editorial team, in practice it is usual to have dedicated staff responsible for the news section of a magazine. For small titles, this may simply consist of a single reporter line-managed directly by the editor, but for magazines where news plays an important factor there may be a news editor running a small team.

The reason for separating news out from other sections is often due to the practicalities of magazine production as much as anything else. Features tend to be less time-specific than reviews which, in turn, go out of date less quickly than news. The production editor will probably be handling a series of deadlines for news stories that are much later in the cycle than those for features.

A good news editor does not merely wait for events to happen, but plans for them in advance. Certain events will affect readers, and while the outcome of these events cannot be known in advance, the fact that they will happen is clear. For example, large companies will make important announcements at major trade shows and may not release information in advance – but the editor knows that he or she needs a reporter there to feed back information.

In addition, writers need to contact industry figures to discover what is going on in the background, and very often PR departments will provide information under embargo, whereby a magazine has the essential facts but cannot report on them until a specified date. Background details to a news story can be written before the time-relevant material is made available.

One important task for the news editor is to encourage his or her staff to build up their contacts book. In addition, close attention should be paid to competitors – not to find out breaking stories (it is too late to do anything about them once they have been published) but to discover the sources that they use for information and to pursue them in future.

The starting point for a lot of stories is the press release, which typically is sent to the news editor. This type of material – increasingly in electronic form – can become overwhelming very easily (and the skill to writing a good press release very often matches that of writing a good news story in that you need to keep your reader engaged).

It is a depressing fact that staff cutbacks on a number of magazines often mean that such releases become the basis of a story – and, indeed, for a short caption story or minor column piece this is not in itself a problem: the magazine is passing on information, usually in a concentrated form, from companies and organisations. However, for bigger stories, such material should be used to provide contacts to follow up for the questions that a magazine's readers want answering – rather than as the opportunity simply for an organisation to tell only the answers that it wants to give.

Features

In contrast to news, which tends to follow a number of fairly clearly defined formulas, magazine features are marked only by their variety. Features can range from short, photo-led articles with long captions (popular in celebrity magazines, for example), to detailed and densely researched articles that run for many pages throughout a title. The only constraint, as Sally Adams (Hicks *et al.* 2008) points out, is to write for the publication and its readers.

Bearing in mind this variety, the main feature formats tend to consist of: profiles (of an individual or group/organisation); product round-ups (of the type commonly found in *Which?* magazine, for example); background features, to put the news in context; and opinion pieces (such as columns, editorials and polemical articles, designed to be provocative to the audience).

The anatomy of a feature

While there is no fixed way to write a feature, many do share some common elements. The notion that a feature has to have a beginning, middle and end is too trite (as we shall see when considering ways of writing intros), but it is rather like a classic short story in that the reader will expect it to be coherent. While the practice of reading news means that we tend to scan stories, taking in as much detail as we consider necessary before moving to the next one, once a reader has committed to a feature story they will be much more likely to read to the end.

The simplest component of a feature, but one that should not be overlooked, is the title. An arresting title, accompanied by an eye-catching graphic, is the first thing that will make someone consider an article interesting enough to read. This is then usually followed by the standfirst, a short introduction that will include some information about the contributor(s) and give an idea of what the article is about. The following are two examples of feature titles and standfirsts:

Smog and Mirrors
Chinese officials have promised to clean up the air for the 2008 Olympics. If banishing power plants and diverting traffic doesn't work, they're willing to shut Beijing down cold. By Spencer Reiss. Photographs by Tony Law.
Wired

Crown of the Continent
By Douglas H. Chadwick. Photographs by Michael Melford. By 2030, Glacier National Park may have lost all its glaciers. But with turquoise lakes, bighorn sheep, and two-mile-high peaks, Glacier-Waterton will always be a wonderland.
National Geographic

Features will nearly always list the writer (unless they are short, caption-led pieces), but not always the photographer. The fact that the two examples above do indicates just how important images are to magazine articles: virtually no one is going to read a feature that consists entirely of text.

Structure and presentation

The presentation of a feature is extremely important for the vast majority of publications. Until the twentieth century, a magazine article looked very similar to a chapter in a book, possibly broken up by the occasional engraved image or divided into columns, but generally consisting of dense text. Innovations in photography and other areas of design, particularly typography, led to a much more experimental approach to presentation.

What should be remembered is the way that most of us read magazines: unlike a novel, where a reader starts at the beginning and works their way through in a linear fashion, most of us begin reading magazines by flicking through them from page to page.

When glancing through different features, the reader's eye is caught by pictures, boxouts, captions and other visual information that can attract him or her to read the rest of the article. And this information is *always* visual: even text is a graphic object, so short blocks of text that stand out in some way may give an insight into the feature that makes us want to read on.

Typical visual devices employed within a feature are:

• Boxes or boxouts, and panels: blocks of text that will be marked off from the main body of the article, for example by being coloured differently to the rest of the page. These can be extremely short – giving a contact address, for example – or short, almost mini-features in their own right that convey a substantial amount of information.

- Bullet points: a simple way of drawing attention to a list of elements within an article.
- Statistical tables: writing out numerical data is the easiest way to lose a reader and makes for very tedious features, whereas the inclusion of a graph or table can get across the point of that information at a glance.
- Information graphics: increasingly popular, particularly in the B2B or more technically minded press, information graphics (such as a map of countries with data on population or diseases) is related to the charts and graphs mentioned above. It may also include such things as cutaways or technical drawings, where information is conveyed to the reader by a combination of image and captions.
- Pull-quotes and captions: these are short extracts of text to illustrate an image or to make the page more visually appealing.

While a feature needs to be coherent, the comparison to a short story is misleading for a number of articles that do not follow a single narrative. It is not uncommon for magazine features to be 'broken up', to consist of a number of separate but related panels each of which provides a single focus for part of the article. For example, a health feature on a particular illness may begin with an introduction, the body copy, which outlines the condition, to be followed by a series of mini-interviews or profiles detailing sufferers and how they cope.

Types of feature

The majority of features that appear in consumer magazines and newspaper supplements are lifestyle features. Many magazines include little else and they may be broken down into the following categories:

- Health and fitness: including that extremely popular staple of women's magazines, the dieting guide, one important crossover that has occurred in the past two decades is the increasing number of fitness guides into general magazines. Whereas these previously were confined to more specialist exercising magazines, a whole range of articles offering advice on exercise appear regularly elsewhere. Health articles may also deal with medical conditions and various treatments and therapies.
- Fashion and beauty: while these two are often intrinsically linked, the beauty element is also often tied to health features. A common way of attracting readers to such articles is to use an interview with a celebrity as the hook or draw for the piece.

- Leisure and hobbies: a rapidly developing sector of the lifestyle market, these titles can be very specialised, with magazines devoted entirely to one particular leisure activity. More often, such articles will cover a particular pursuit in more general titles.
- Relationships and sex: extremely popular in men's and women's titles, articles dealing with these subjects can range from the relatively innocuous, such as flirting with the opposite sex, to fairly graphic accounts of what to do in bed, or more complex articles that will focus on a psychological aspect of relationships.
- Homes and gardens: the boom in house prices in the past decade has contributed to the rise of a huge number of articles and magazines that deal with such things as home improvement tips and celebrity properties.
- Food: incorporating cooking and restaurant reviews, this is a long-established genre for general as well as specialist titles.
- Travel: travel features can consist of those that offer specific guidance on visiting places (accommodation, things to do and so on), and ones that focus more on telling a narrative about the writer's visit to a particular place or, increasingly, focusing on an aspect of the travel industry.
- Family: including the sub-category of babies and parenting, these articles will focus on relationships between family members, usually from a psychological point of view, or offer practical advice.
- The arts: in some ways a distinct category of lifestyle journalism, and a diverse one that tends to lend itself very well to reviewing, it includes articles on art, books, music, drama and film.

In addition to this general category of lifestyle features, a great many articles – particularly those that deal with celebrity or fame in some way – are based around a profile or interview. The writer is expected to conduct an in-depth interview with their subject, and for an effective article will have to engage in research before the meeting to ensure that he or she asks all the right questions, and does not simply repeat what has been published before. In addition, the profile should have an angle, a purpose that will make the audience want to read it. For example, a profile of an actor or band should be related to a new movie or album that is being released.

For the journalist conducting the interview, the craft is to convert what will almost certainly be far too much material (usually captured on tape or a digital recorder) into a compelling and coherent narrative. An article that is packed with too many quotes can actually become quite boring to read, so usually the majority of information will be reported as indirect speech, converting long quotations to single sentences and allowing more space for background information on the interviewee. Another point to bear in mind when writing such pieces is whether they are written in the first person ('X told me') or the third person, where no mention is made of the writer at all.

Another category that is a popular staple of features is the opinion or comment piece: nearly all magazines will have an editorial, whereby an editor seeks to offer his or her opinion on a subject that affects readers, but many more also include such things as gossip columns, diaries and 'op-ed' comment pieces. The talents required for such features can be varied: a gossip columnist needs to be interested in people – indeed, generally very nosy – while the opinion writer must be willing to adopt strong opinions to try to rouse the audience.

Comment pieces may merge with background or news features, particularly if investigating a subject that is potentially contentious in the spheres of business, politics, environment and so on. The point of such articles is to provide more detailed analysis of events going on in the world that will appeal to readers, and significant levels of research are needed to make such a feature authoritative and compelling.

The product round-up, also known as consumer journalism, is very common in certain types of magazine and rarely dealt with at all in others. Motoring and computer titles, for example, will often run features that compare certain types of car or PC, and the leading title in this regard is *Which?*, which regularly reviews everything from mortgages to washing machines.

Even more general lifestyle magazines may include consumer 'tests' of such things as make-up products or clothes. At the more professional end, however, a serious consumer title will have a set of standards against which a product can be tested (for example, fuel efficiency, handling and comfort for a particular car).

Such articles are avidly read by advertisers as well as consumers, and it is not uncommon for the former to try to influence the outcome of a particular test. However, any magazine that is serious about such journalism – which is becoming increasingly important in helping the reader select goods from a bewildering range of choices – will maintain strict controls over the role of manufacturers who provide goods for testing. In the USA, as with *Which?* in the UK, it is not unknown for magazine editors to purchase the goods they test in order to prevent any undue influence.

Style and content

The starting point for any feature writer is to think of the audience; although the article can (and should) be immensely creative, there is a significant difference between the creative writing associated with fiction and journalistic writing for magazines, key to which are the expectations of readers who regularly consume a particular title. An article for *The Economist* is obviously going to read very differently from one for *Heat*, and the writer must take into account the demographics and background of the audience.

Associated with this is finding the right voice. Some magazines regularly publish features written in the first voice, not necessarily that of the journalist: real-life titles, which have become very popular in recent years, for example, will offer the story of a member of the public told from their point of view, although the material is drawn from interviews and then structured into a finished article by the writer.

Similarly, opinion pieces will often offer a very forceful voice of the person writing the feature (although this itself, when it works well, is a carefully constructed version of aspects of the journalist's personality). When applied wrongly, however, such writing can seem egocentric and inappropriate, and background features, for example, work best when told from the position of an impersonal, third-person narrator.

Deciding which tense to write a story in – past or present – can have a significant effect on the impact of a story. Features written in the present tense can appear much more vivid, but the danger is the temptation to slip into the past tense, which is a more natural way of presenting amounts of information about events that have been completed.

Similarly, the type of vocabulary used should be appropriate to the audience: while jargon is best avoided at all times, if you are writing a feature for a very tightly focused audience in a specific industry, say, then failing to use commonly employed terminology will make your writing seem amateurish. Even so, the long sentences and complex language associated with certain professions such as the law and academia are never appropriate outside specialised journals.

Writing intros

With the standfirst, the intro is the hook that draws the reader into the rest of the article. Although techniques for writing intros to features are nowhere near as prescriptive as those for news stories, they should be written with the rest of the story in mind. In particular, it is important to establish the angle of your piece – whether it is a factual, news-based piece or something that draws upon 'softer' features.

Of the various types of introduction to a magazine article, commonly used ones include anecdotes or descriptions, which set the scene by describing a person or place or tell a story related to the main subject of the feature. Consider the following from a recent *Guardian Weekend* profile of Mackenzie Crook, star of the *Pirates of the Caribbean* movies and TV sitcom *The Office*:

> My wife recently bought a pedometer. You're meant to take 10,000 steps a day, and I did 15,000 just in an average day at home. I pace all the time. I can't sit still and watch a film on TV. I have to do stuff. Constantly on the move.

The point for anyone who has seen Mackenzie is that this anecdote, which has nothing to do with the ostensible purpose of the feature (a review of the actor's career at the time of the release of *Pirates of the Caribbean 3*), is immediately meant to explain his unconventional appearance. It also serves to reinforce the angle of the piece – that Mackenzie's subsequent Hollywood career has been little short of astonishing – by suggesting a deeper drive that cannot, literally, sit still.

Other techniques for opening an article include the provocative statement or question that is meant to intrigue the reader. These should make the reader think, or rouse his opinions strongly for or against the opening statement. For example, Joe Klein began one of his *Time* magazine columns during the 2004 presidential election as follows: 'Bush's argument is tight, concise and, so far, impregnable. It is also a clever distortion of reality.' Considering the divisions in the USA at the time, the beauty of such a statement was that both Republicans and Democrats would find something to disagree with.

Finally, the old stop-gap if you are really stuck for an opening is to use a quotation. Although often dismissed as lazy journalism, a carefully selected quote from your interviewee can intrigue, provoke or stimulate the reader to continue with the rest of the piece.

The role of the features editor

The position of features editor is one of the most interesting on a magazine. For larger titles, as with the news editor, he or she will probably be responsible for a number of staff writers, and share similar responsibilities in terms of ensuring that copy is prepared for a particular section of a magazine. It is more likely, however, that the features editor will work with a number of freelance writers: the demands of deadlines tend to be looser for features and, in addition, the editor is more likely to need a wider range of expertise and experience for different types of article.

Although the tendency throughout this chapter has been to talk of a generic features editor, on many titles the need to produce longer articles tends to create not one but several editors, each with responsibility for a different type of content. Thus there may be a lifestyle editor, fashion editor, food and homes editor on a women's title, each working with different writers and freelances to produce content for the title. For all such editors, an important part of their job is to generate ideas for forthcoming issues – to do which they must keep an eye on the competition, develop expertise in their area of responsibility and talk to industry experts as much as possible.

Reviews

Along with news and features, reviews are a staple of many magazines, both consumer titles and B2B. A substantial proportion of titles are taken up with reviews in some shape or form, reflecting the fact that many of us buy magazines not simply to be entertained or be informed as to what is happening in the world, but also to receive advice on the bewildering array of objects and events that face us as consumers.

So, what is a review? On a very superficial level, a review tends to be longer than a news story and shorter than a feature – but this does not really define reviews. Indeed, some very effective review writing may consist of short and pithy paragraphs that convey the writer's opinion in a few lines. And this is key to a review: it must provide the writer's opinion; a critical assessment of what he or she thought of the subject under scrutiny.

A review is not simply a listing, something that conveys information about events or other topics in as neutral a fashion as possible. In addition to this, the writer has to describe what they are reviewing, whether it is a film, a meal at a restaurant or a financial service, and then offer an assessment of whether they believe it to be suitable or not.

This, in turn, raises a number of questions regarding the experience of the reviewer, which often relate to implicit opinions that he or she holds regarding the subject under review. What are the values that the reviewer uses to base judgements upon? At some level, these will come from an awareness of what else is happening in the field. For example, making the statement that something is too expensive should come from the knowledge of how much similar items are sold for elsewhere.

In a modern consumer society, reviewing provides a service. Readers are faced with immense choice, and often do not have the experience to make reasonable comparisons. This is what they look for in the reviews, and so good review writing (which is not by any means the same as a good, in the sense of favourable, review) needs to spell out what people need to know about goods and services.

Ultimately, the reader will need to make up his or her own mind – and nowhere is this clearer than in matters of taste, such as film or music reviews. The cliché may be that 'everyone hates a critic', but if the critic provides an honest and thoughtful appraisal the truth is they might respect the opinion if not the person.

The qualifications to be a reviewer

In the second act of Samuel Beckett's *Waiting for Godot*, the two principal characters Vladimir and Estragon launch into a series of insults against each other. After trading various terms of abuse such as 'moron', 'abortion', 'sewer-rat' and 'cretin', Estragon hurls the word 'Crritic' (rolled around his mouth 'with finality', we are told), causing Vladimir to visibly wilt, vanquished.

Drama has a rich tradition of insulting theatre critics, mainly because reviewers can be so damning of the plays that they see. One of the most common retorts to a bad review is to challenge the critic to put on a play. The idea is that once they realise just how difficult it is to direct and produce for the stage, they will be more sympathetic, but behind this is another assumption: that to understand a subject properly, you have to be a practitioner.

The ferocity with which theatre reviews are often rebuffed is probably due to the fact that although directing and acting require specific skills, the drama critic could potentially be seen as a failed dramatist. (Something similar occurs in literary reviewing, which is another often very vicious arena where publications such as the *London Review of Books* appear to delight in giving a book to a writer who was previously trashed in its pages by the very author of the book under review.)

In most other areas, however, such potential crossovers are rare. It is highly unlikely that the film critic will ever be able to amass the budget required to release a motion picture, and the automobile reviewer will not be employed to design cars. Yet, is there any truth in the notion that better reviews are provided by those who practise the craft they are examining? Should music reviews be written by musicians? Should we leave the appraisal of buildings to architects? And is there a role for well-written food reviews in the hands of anyone other than a top chef?

The last example may be the best one in drawing attention to what it is a reviewer does: not all of us can cook – and only a very few of us can cook exceptionally well. Yet all of us can eat, and if not everyone can eat well the task that a good reviewer sets him- or herself is often to educate the tastes (in this case literally) of the reader. And this is the most important point: the critic must write first and foremost for the reader, not the producer.

So a reviewer does not need to be a practitioner; indeed, in some areas it may be a hindrance. We want our best chefs to concentrate on their culinary skills, and while there are notable exceptions, a certain degree of verbal inadequacy is not necessarily a hindrance to producing great rock music. A reviewer, after all, is a writer, and it is in writing that his or her particular skill lies.

Despite this, the ability to produce good reviews does require a considerable amount of knowledge and expertise in a field, as well as enthusiasm for the subject. If you have no interest in film, then the chances are that your writing about the movies will be a lacklustre affair. In addition, you are hardly likely to engage with the history and background of film in such a way as to give you a solid base for comparing new releases. A reviewer does not need to *do*, but he or she does need to *understand*.

With regard to writing for the reader, another important aspect to bear in mind, as with other types of journalistic copy, is the audience for that particular magazine. Technical reviews work well when the readership of a title is technically minded, presumably because they share a similar professional background. For other markets, the reviewer will often need to provide simpler explanations, although even writing for a more specialised audience should always be clear and direct.

Structure of a review

The first step to writing a review must be to determine your opinion of the topic under consideration – whether it is good, bad or indifferent. In order to determine that, you must of course first note down your experience, approaching the subject with as open a mind as possible. If you have decided in advance that something is wonderful or atrocious, it is unlikely you will write a fair review (more on which later).

For busy staff writers, reviews might, unfortunately, be written on the hoof to hit imminent deadlines. Ideally, however, the reviewer should spend time preparing their piece as much as possible: a little research can go a long way. Before dealing with sense impressions, the reviewer must establish the facts, such as whether this is the first album by a band, or the price on the road of a new car.

When writing up a review, most magazines have a fairly clear format as to presentation, some elements of which will probably be quite rigid. A large number will have some form of rating system, whether stars out of five or ten or something more unusual, and it is typical to have a boxout or short section that provides a quick summary of the item and the reviewer's opinions.

For other elements of a review, the writer needs to decide where to provide such things as factual information (near the beginning, as the reader is unlikely to know much about the subject), and how much description to give before moving on to his or her verdict.

Fair comment, libel and malicious falsehood

Expressing an opinion is the most important part of the review – and something which is often restricted by the demands of a word count, so that it can be difficult to justify your estimation as deeply as you would like. Examples should be given, not merely to avoid dull statements, but which will also indicate the writer's own taste (and allow the audience to disagree).

The issue of libel and malicious falsehood will be discussed in greater detail in Chapter 7, but it is an issue that can greatly affect review writers because so often derogatory comments will appear in print or online. If the reviewer truly believes that a product or service is poor, then he or she must say so – but no critic is immune to libel laws.

In the UK, the USA and many European countries, the right to publish an honest opinion – under what is known as 'fair comment' – means that a reviewer has the right to be as unfair as he or she likes as long as this is their true opinion. However, getting facts wrong (even if this is an 'honest' mistake) is no defence, and if opinion is seen as over the top or maliciously motivated, this too can lead to a libel prosecution.

At the other end of the scale, the fear of libel, as well as a sometimes pernicious influence of advertisers in publications that fear losing out on any advertising, can result in bland and boring reviews. It is probably going a little too far to describe it as the reviewer's *duty* to publish his or her honest opinion, but if the alternative is dull and tedious copy it is certainly a service to the reader to write what they think.

The role of the reviews editor

The reviews editor, when employed on a sizable title, will have similar responsibilities in many respects to the news and features editors, having to manage a team and provide ideas for forthcoming issues.

Something that can be substantially different, especially for those magazines in which reviews of goods play an important role, is that the editor will also need to organise some way of dealing with incoming items. Many magazines are sent lots of items for review, and the editor will have to put in place a system for getting these to freelances or staff writers, and ensuring that expensive goods are returned to the appropriate manufacturer.

For some titles that deal with particularly complicated items, such as computers or electronic goods, there may even need to be some sort of 'lab'. In many cases, this could simply be part of a room set aside to test equipment, but alongside it there will be some sort of set of tests that will provide for equal treatment of products from different producers.

Commissioning

While commissioning freelance writers is sometimes treated as a black art, the essentials are generally straightforward: commissioning editors (usually a section editor) will have to negotiate with a writer within the constraints of an editorial budget. The amount available will probably vary from month to month, as some magazines have different amounts of editorial in different issues, but the commissioning editor will need to know what is available to him or her.

The next step is to determine levels of payment: typically, freelances are paid per 1,000 words, and for some titles there will be a fixed fee, but others will vary the amounts paid depending on whether they wish to attract certain, more experienced writers. Yet others will always require some degree of negotiation or, say when hiring freelances to cover an important event for which no staff writers are available, a day fee, including expenses.

Writing a brief

When a commissioning editor has located suitable writers, and before any negotiations take place, he or she will need to provide them with a brief. As the name suggests, this should be concise but also comprehensive, outlining what the editor expects the freelance to do, including any angle to be taken, specific content that may be required and additional features to be included in the article such as boxouts or panels. For some titles, the writer may also be required to provide pictures or graphics.

The brief will also need to include a deadline, which is not the deadline for publication but, rather, when copy needs to be returned to the magazine so that it can be subbed and laid out appropriately. Writers will almost certainly wish to know, however, when a piece will appear, particularly if payment is to be made 30 days after publication. In addition, some articles will require a very specific word count to fill a particular space, while others will be the average required for a certain number of pages; if the writer over-writes, the fee remains the same.

The final question to be determined (after delivery – usually email these days, at least for copy) is rights. Copyright will be discussed more fully in Chapter 7, but one thing to bear in mind when commissioning is the distinction between First British Serial Rights, the right to publish once in a British newspaper or magazine, and full rights for redistribution internationally or via another medium such as the web. Typically, publishers will ask for a writer to 'assign', or sell, the copyright, or will demand an unlimited licence to redistribute the writer's copyrighted work in different media.

In the second half of the 1990s, particularly as the internet was becoming an ever more popular medium, this approach caused considerable consternation among freelances. In practice, very little written work (as opposed to images, where it still remains contentious) is re-sold, but an editor may need to exercise sensitivity, particularly when dealing with a famous or well-established writer. Today, as digital is increasingly the first point of distribution, this has become a non-issue for most journalists.

Rewrites and kill fees

Sometimes an article will be unusable, sometimes because of a fault on the part of the magazine (for example, pages have been cut because not enough ads have been sold), but more often than not because the writer has not produced what the editor expected. Strictly speaking, a kill fee is payment made to close a contract before the commission is completed, but more usually it is made after copy comes in and it cannot be used in the title.

Obviously, if the work is completely unprofessional then the writer can be seen to have failed to fulfil his part of the contract and so does not deserve payment (although obviously the writer may see things very differently). More often, although there are problems with a piece the writer may still be useful for future work. In these cases, a kill fee is the most suitable way to close the commission. These should be used sparingly, however; not only are they simply a waste of money that could be better spent elsewhere, but such payments are likely to sour relations in some way between the magazine and the freelance.

Alternatively, if a piece can be salvaged, it is perfectly reasonable to ask for a rewrite under the terms of the original commission. If the article is still to appear in the same issue of the magazine, obviously the turn-around for such a piece will be very tight. In addition, the editor is then committed to paying a full fee even if the piece is not used – in which case it may be simpler to pay a kill fee and have it rewritten in-house.

Finally, when sent a piece 'on spec', the editor must make it very clear that this is simply being considered – it has not been commissioned and so, if it is not used, no fee is paid.

Freelances versus staff writers

The issues around rights draw attention to one distinction between using freelance writers and in-house staff: under British law, staff writers have no copyright over their own material, so copy produced in such a way can be re-used as the editor sees fit. Indeed, the potential for conflict that emerged in the 1990s did see a movement away from relying on small numbers of staff and a larger stable of freelances, although this has become much less of an issue in recent years.

There are, however, other times when it is better to use staff writers. Some articles (and news stories feature very highly in this way) require a considerable amount of work and research to produce a small amount of copy. Staff writers can pursue such things as phone calls from the office as they do other tasks during the day.

Likewise, if an editor wishes to try a new type of feature, which may or may not end up being used in a magazine, it is better to use somebody already employed by the title than potentially waste money commissioning a freelance. Similarly, if a project is particularly sensitive, in most cases a staff journalist should be employed so that competitors do not know what is being planned.

Yet no substantial magazine will rely entirely on staffers; for variety in terms of writing, as well as the need to call on different levels of expertise, all editors will seek to maintain a contact list of freelances that they can call on to provide copy.

Subbing

For many students working on a magazine project for the last time, the temptation is to view layout as the last stage of the production cycle, with sub-editing viewed as a necessary evil that can be skipped over as quickly as possible. Yet subbing is a valuable skill that is essential to professional magazine production, so valuable in fact that editors often have a harder time recruiting suitable sub-editors than they do getting decent journalists to fill a staff-writing role.

At its most basic level, sub-editing involves quality control, looking for factual errors, typos or literals and solecisms to ensure that everything is accurate and well written. As well as this, the sub-editor plays an important role in the production cycle by ensuring that copy fits both in terms of its layout on the page and with a house style. For many titles subs also have the job of thinking up titles and standfirsts for articles (although on others this is an editor's task), and nearly all will expect them to provide such things as captions for images.

When dealing with copy, the first thing that a sub must do is focus on clarity to make sure the article is readable for the magazine audience. While journalists may be very close to their sources, often adding too much detail and even writing in jargon, subs will often wish to simplify and explain – although plain English is not the same as dull language. It is for this reason that subbing always has to be done by another person: while a writer can check his or her own copy for mistakes, what they have written will nearly always be meaningful to them. For the sub, however, this will be the first encounter with copy that, if it is not clear, may need changing.

Regarding inaccuracies, these fall into two types. First of all there are mistakes of spelling, grammar and syntax. The second type consists of factual errors, which might need to be rectified by a phone call or checking another source. Too many of the former make a publication appear unprofessional to the reader; the latter might go unnoticed by most readers but can have more serious consequences, especially if they lead to inadvertently libellous statements. Potentially contentious statements should be referred to an editor.

Such activities, while important, do not themselves make substantial changes to the text. However, when dealing with an art department that will provide a layout, the sub-editor's job also consists of making copy fit the page, and in some cases this can involve considerable adjustments. Text may need to be cut or even expanded, and if these are more than minor, an editor, and probably the author, should be informed (and asked to rewrite): this is one area where a sub can inadvertently introduce his or her own mistakes. In addition, captions, pull-quotes and other additional visual elements need to be added.

Where other changes may take place is with regard to the house style. Any magazine that uses a range of writers will have a variety of voices – as, indeed, it should – to prevent articles becoming too monotonous. However, some degree of uniformity should be imposed across a magazine. In some cases, this will be minor issues of style, such as whether to use digits or words for small numbers ('6' as opposed to 'six'), or terms of address when required. In other cases, there may be certain ways that a magazine likes to refer to topics that are regularly covered, or it may have a style that is informal or formal for various subjects.

SEO

In recent years, the issue of how readers find articles to read has changed dramatically for magazine brands. Prior to the widespread use of the web, magazine publishers had to appeal to potential consumers on the newsstand and, as we shall see in the next chapter, a front cover is still extremely important. Today, however, it is increasingly likely that readers will come to a feature, review or news story via a search engine which makes SEO incredibly important.

Because an article's ranking in a search engine such as Google or Bing is so important, entire careers have been built and vast amounts of virtual ink have been spilt on the subject. Very often, the more convoluted attempts to improve that rank consist of attempts to trick search engines through potentially duplicitous means – and companies such as Google are constantly refining their sites to remove false leads that come, for example, from poorly employed keywords or links from spurious sites.

A search engine works in two main ways. First bots or web crawlers, sophisticated pieces of software, search the web, going from link to link and retrieving this to the host's databases where they are indexed. This is important because when you access a site such as Google or Bing, you are not actually searching the entire web (which would take a long time) but rather the company's database which is then linked to the original page. Google states that as of early 2016 its index is over 100,000,000 gigabytes in size and has been amassed over a million computing hours.

Because the search host uses its own database, it can then refine the visitor's search using algorithms. These may take obvious forms, such as auto-suggest or auto-complete, which are often based on the most popular previous searches. They can also be more subtle, such as correcting spelling mistakes, or making use of knowledge graphs to plot a current search against what people have looked for previously in order to guess the best answers. As such, no web search is 'cold', simply trawling the web as it exists now to find all responses to a particular term.

Finally, search engines are very keen to deal with spam and junk. Spam sites attempt to get to the top of search ranking systems which results in relevant pages falling down the list, and search engines will look out for obviously bot-generated sites which are often gibberish to a reader or scrape content from other, legitimate pages. Search engines also tend not to favour sites stuffed with irrelevant keywords, which was often a means by which SEO spammers attempted to improve their ratings.

Working with SEO

With this brief introduction to SEO in mind, the final part of this chapter offers some advice on writing with search engines in mind. The difficulty for a journalist is to produce content that will be clear enough to be ranked by a web site, but also witty, intriguing and appealing enough to be read by a person. There is no need to follow an infamous 2006 headline from *The New York Times*: 'This Boring Headline is Written for Google'.

The most important thing to remember is the need for clarity; despite the advances in computing in recent years, humans still tend to handle ambiguity better than machines – but then most of us aren't trawling millions of web pages every hour. As such, deciding the primary topic of your story is important in helping you define your keywords.

Keywords used to be the primary focus for SEO in terms of arcane instructions for applying them via meta tags and other HTML elements, but as search engines increasingly concentrate on the content on a page (to avoid 'keyword stuffing' which is a common tactic of spam sites), it's more helpful to think of keywords as the primary topics for your article. These then should appear in your title and page content near the beginning and, ideally, in any descriptions of the page. If, as Kim Brooks wrote for *Salon* in 2014, you are going to write about leaving your son in a car, there's not a much better headline than 'The Day I Left My Son in the Car'. This particular one works well for both machines and people.

Another important place for keywords is in images. While search engines have improved considerably in recent years when it comes to recognising visual elements, in the end it is still much easier to search through words. Some of this can be dealt with via tags attached to images, but even for those who have no knowledge of HTML it is always useful to include a clear, descriptive caption.

Links are an important means to improve your rank. Search engines often rate content by how many other web sites link back to the host, and in the end building up good links requires you to write compelling content. One short cut, however, which is useful for all magazine editors is to provide plenty of (relevant) internal links on a page to other parts of the brand's site. You should also link to other web sites with related content and, where possible, encourage sites to link back as this will improve your ratings.

When producing a magazine site, one important element is to move away from a content management system that uses permalinks based on numbers to one based on words that, again, can be searched by a web crawler. 'Mysite.com/jacks-article/' is much better than 'mysite.com/?p=25346'.

Finally, while you may produce the ultimate web page that hits the top of a search ranking system immediately, if your site as a whole is not updated regularly that ranking will only decay with time. To remain at the top of the heap, sites need to be updated regularly.

5
Designing for print

While the verbal content that goes into an article is extremely important, providing the matter that will entertain and inform readers for the hours that they choose to read a magazine, the visual content cannot and should not be considered at all inferior. Since the invention of photography, and the revolutions in design and print technologies that occurred in the early twentieth century and again after the Second World War, the way magazines *look* has become essential to their appeal to readers.

Throughout the last century, magazines have evolved to be an almost perfect medium for photography in particular, and since the 1970s and 1980s certainly most consumer publications have moved to glossy production values which show off visuals to the best effect. Good magazine design is a combination of illustration, typography and colour, all of which must be joined together into an effective layout.

The role of the production editor

The production editor is the final key role in terms of magazine production. On smaller magazines, the position may be taken by the editor, but for larger titles there will be a separate production editor whose task is to ensure that all deadlines are met and that all stages of the workflow progress as smoothly as possible.

While the strategy of editorial planning is the responsibility of the editor (which is why it was introduced in Chapter 4), day-to-day maintenance of the flat-plan will fall under the remit of the production editor. He or she provides a strong link between the editorial and art departments, ensuring that copy is passed on for layout and then on to sub-editors (for whom he or she will have managerial responsibility).

As well as working with the sections of a magazine responsible for words and visuals, the production editor will have to liaise with the advertising department. As pointed out in Chapter 4, the flat-plan does not simply include editorial pages but also the position of ads, and films or files for these will need to come in at set deadlines to be passed on to the printer.

This leads to the final major responsibility of the production editor: to engage with the printer. The production editor will need to collect mechanical data from the printer (page sizes and file types, for example) and ensure that the relevant material is ready to go to press, whether film or digital files.

The role of the art editor

The art editor's role is vital to the success of the magazine – indeed, alongside that of the publisher and the editor is probably the most important as to how it is received in the market. Because the visual impact will affect readers so immediately, this can have a great effect on circulation, so the art editor and editor will need to work in close conjunction.

As well as coming up with ideas for design and illustration him- or herself, the art editor will be responsible for a team of layout artists and designers if working for a sizeable publication. The role is also one of the most significant in terms of commissioning: the art editor has to build up a stable of freelances who can provide photography and illustration, and while some of this can probably be done in-house the chances are that it will come from external sources.

For some titles where famous or proprietary images have to be sourced on a regular basis, there may be a separate picture editor, but on most titles this will be another responsibility of the art editor, or one that he or she delegates to a member of the design team.

As well as being expected to provide a coherent design for the entire magazine, the single most important page that the art editor has to take responsibility for is the cover, as this is what will attract or turn off readers at the newsstand. As part of the job, he or she will have to think up new ideas – working alongside the editor and production department (who typically think up the cover lines) to ensure that this has the greatest possible impact.

The tendency of most consumer magazines today has, rather depressingly, been to rely on a single photograph of an individual. While some of these can still have a remarkable effect (and seem to be expected by most readers), it does mean that there is less space than ever before for expressing abstract ideas through the cover. Obviously there are exceptions – such as computer and car magazines, although even these tend to rely on stock images of the products they cover. Ironically, it is probably in some sectors of the B2B press that the most imaginative approach has been taken to presenting abstract cover ideas in recent years.

In addition to managing the in-house studio and dealing with freelances, the final managerial task of the art editor is to work with external agencies that will provide some elements of printing and colour work. While much of this will fall into the remit of the production editor, dealt with in the next chapter, this can take up a substantial amount of the art editor's time and budget.

Impact versus beauty

Most designers will probably wish to produce a magazine that is a beautiful aesthetic object – but beauty is very much in the eye of the beholder and a subjective value that does not always work best towards particular designs. As Morrish (2003) observes, for many titles beauty is a far too static ideal and what a good designer works towards is *impact*.

This can be very evident in some of the best-selling titles in the UK, European and American markets, some of which look garish by any standards. Notions such as harmonising colours or selecting subtle images and logos appear to have been discarded, to be replaced by bright, neon lettering on brash, day-glo colours. And yet the designs of these magazines work – battling it out on the front line of the newsstand to attract notoriously promiscuous readers who flit from title to title each week.

Of course, when chasing a mass market, the design techniques for such titles have to be loud and rather kitsch. But titles that do not seek such wide circulation will obviously wish to announce very different values in terms of design. Using more restrained colours and balanced designs, titles such as *Vogue* and *Wallpaper** wish to indicate to both advertisers and readers that they are much classier than the tabloids.

Working with designers

In the vast majority of cases, layout will typically be done in-house. This makes most sense as pages need to be modified or amended on a day-by-day basis, and all but the smallest editorial team will have graphic designers either dedicated to their magazine, or part of a centralised art team. Very small magazines might commission a designer to provide a template which is then filled in with copy and photos by the editor or an editorial assistant.

For photography and illustration, while some elements of these will be done in-house it is more likely that much of the work will be done by freelances. As with written features, composing an accompanying illustration for an article can be too time-consuming for layout artists who have to get pages ready for print.

Similarly with photography, not only can a photo shoot be quite protracted, but a professional photographer will fulfil all the requirements for studio and equipment. In addition, while photographs make up a huge proportion of the content of most magazines it is usually only for short periods of time during the production cycle that the editor needs to concentrate on photography. It is much more sensible to hire freelances, or for multi-title companies to hire photographers who work across several magazines.

On some titles, for example those that deal with celebrity, the freelance has become essential in his or her most notorious form: as a member of the paparazzi. Elsewhere, the number of freelance photographers employed by magazines simply draws attention to the fact that no staff member can hope to be in every place all of the time.

This is a situation that is very different to the regional (if not national) press. For a long time it had been the custom on local newspapers to employ one or more photographers who would go out with reporters to take pictures for the daily paper. With tight deadlines, this made sense. Increasingly, however, at least for smaller offices, reporters themselves are expected to take a digital camera with them. On newsprint, an editor can get away with this (particularly as the photos were always unlikely to be of studio quality anyway); the visual impact of glossies means that there are no chances of this happening in the vast majority of magazines.

For the rest of this chapter, I will consider the various elements that go into magazine design before concentrating on bringing them together in a page layout.

Text and typography

So far, this book has dealt with the style and content of text from the point of view of writers and editors, but, as has already been mentioned, text also functions in a magazine as part of the design. Columns and blocks of text, combined with such things as boxes and pull-quotes, create a dynamic design that will draw the eye into the page as the reader moves from small, concentrated snippets of information such as a picture caption into the main body of the article.

What is more, in all but the dullest of magazine designs, text has to work in conjunction with other graphic elements, particularly photographs or illustrations and also colour on the page.

Fonts and typefaces

Although the terms font and typeface are often used interchangeably, a type-face was traditionally a complete set of characters in multiple fonts and sizes, while a font was a typeface in one size and style, such as italic or bold. It is common usage today to employ font (or, more rarely, fount) to mean typeface, and that is how the word will be used throughout the rest of this chapter.

As well as italic and bold, font styles also include Roman (the standard, or default, script for word processors), bold italic, condensed, extended and small capitals. There are several others, but these are the ones most commonly used in print. In the UK and USA, type size is measured in points, with approx-imately 72 points to the inch. Another method, used in mainland Europe, is the didot system, where type is measured in ciceros.

One thing to bear in mind is that while there is a wide range of point sizes familiar to any user of a word processor, typically 8 to 72, the actual print sizes of different fonts are not exactly the same (which is why, for example, 10 point Arial looks bigger than 10 point Times New Roman).

Obviously, font size has an important part to play in page design, with larger text catching the reader's eye more quickly than small text, and setting different parts of the page in different type sizes will build up its own logic of how to read the page. A headline in a large font will be read first, and small captions or text at the end of the article indicates to the reader that he or she does not need to look at this to understand the content on the page.

At the same time, font styles will also change the way the reader approaches the page. Captions, for example, will typically be in a smaller font size than body text, yet by placing them in bold the reader's eye will be drawn to them more quickly. Similarly, use of italics is the most common way to emphasise text, but sometimes the use of a different face such as SMALL CAPS can have a more dramatic impact.

Legibility and experimentation

While there is much more that can be written on the use of typography (with Frost's *Designing for Newspapers and Magazines* providing a good introduction to this subject), here I shall limit myself to just a couple more pointers that should be considered by anyone designing a magazine page.

The first point is that modern computer programs such as QuarkXPress and Adobe InDesign provide access to a potentially bewildering array of different typefaces such as Baskerville Old Face and Monotype Corsica. Students experimenting for the first time with typography are often tempted to try out as many of these fonts as possible, but there is a very good reason why most print is restricted to a handful of faces: legibility.

In contrast to posters and covers, where there is plenty of room for experimentation, the majority of magazines still consist of large sections of print, and attempting to read anything over an extended period of time in a kooky typeface becomes a chore for the reader. Even worse is the tendency to mix a large number of typefaces on a page – a particularly heinous crime if it is done within body text. At best, a designer will restrict him- or herself to three or four different typefaces to clearly mark out separate design elements, such as headings, subheadings, captions and body text.

The second point is the distinction between serif and sans serif fonts. When writing with quills, letters formed thick and thin strokes, which remain in many modern fonts as little curlicues on the end of each letter. Sans serif fonts do not have these small flourishes, and became popular in the twentieth century

Helvetica sans serif font

Bodoni MT serif font

Figure 5.1 Sans serif and serif fonts

as a more 'modern' typeface design. In practice, serif fonts seem to be preferred by most readers as more legible and so used for large sections of body text, with sans serif used for headings and covers because individual letters stand out more clearly.

Fonts and print

When using fonts in certain programs, particularly earlier versions of QuarkXPress, it should always be borne in mind that there may be issues of compatibility between one computer system (that used by the publisher) and another (that used by the printer). While the move to PDF and embedding fonts (see the next chapter) means that this is much less of a problem than previously, in some cases it is still necessary to provide any unusual fonts that may be used in a design on disk to a printer. Without this, the program may revert to a default font (such as Helvetica or Times) that ruins the page design.

There are different font technologies used for screen displays and print, but the most common ones are TrueType, Postscript Type 1 and OpenType. Postscript Type 1 is the older digital format, devised by Adobe in 1985 and still commonly used. These fonts contain only some information embedded in the font itself, while the rest must be handled by Adobe Type Manager (included with most Adobe programs or part of MacOS X). This often distinguishes between a screen font, displayed on the computer monitor, and a print font which is actually handled by a compatible printer.

TrueType, designed by Apple and Microsoft in 1990, includes all information about the font in the font file itself. Postscript is still very popular for commercial printing because Adobe software has become so popular and is built into high-end printers, but there is less scope for error when printing with TrueType.

OpenType, developed more recently by Adobe in conjunction with Microsoft, works on the TrueType format but also includes Postscript information that can extend the character set (to include more letters beyond the usual limits of the font) and advanced typographic controls.

Leading, kerning and justification

As well as type size, the presentation of text on a page is affected by leading (pronounced 'ledding') and kerning, essentially the space between lines and between letters.

Leading, which takes its name from the strips of lead that were used by printers to separate rows of type, is the white space between lines of text. Setting the same font size in different leading sizes can have an impact on how we read a page. Setting font size and leading size to the same amount usually makes text look too cramped, while increasing the latter by as little as two points (say 12 point leading for a 10 point font) can dramatically improve legibility. Increasing leading even more can give a light, airy feel to a page – very useful if that is the impression you wish to convey, less so if you want your page to look busy.

Kerning refers to the process of adjusting the space between letters. Just as individual letters can vary in vertical size, with ascenders and descenders helping to distinguish letters such as 'b' and 'p', so the width of letters such as 'l' and 'w' can be very different. A monotype font, such as Courier, gives exactly the same amount of space to each letter, and looks less appealing aesthetically than kerned fonts, which increase or decrease the space between letters.

Kerning is largely handled automatically by modern software, but occasionally – particularly when designing a cover – the art editor may wish to make manual changes. This is because certain combinations of letters can look slightly odd, with a little too much or too little white space between them.

Justification refers to the alignment of text, with fully justified text being aligned on both the left- and right-hand sides of the page or column. Usually in magazines and newspapers, text is only justified on the left and allowed to run 'ragged right', with lines being uneven on the right-hand side of the column. In contrast to most books, where text is nearly always fully justified, leaving one side ragged improves legibility in body copy arranged in columns.

Text presentation

When arranging text graphically on the page, there are several devices that can be used to make it more visually appealing before even considering such things as illustrations or colour.

When dealing with statistical information, or a series of lists, text is much easier to read when tabulated (arranged into a table). The eye moves easily from one column to the next and the reader can take in at a glance data that would be confusing when presented in the form of sentences.

Drop letters or drop caps are large initial letters at the beginning of an article or section heading. These can be a very simple way to draw the reader's attention to where they should start reading, or to indicate a break in the body copy. Visually, as well, they add interest and flair to a page when used judiciously.

Subheadings, or crossheads, or short lines of text between certain paragraphs, again provide visual interest to an article. They are also useful to the reader (and often the writer) in helping to structure a piece: occasional subheadings help to indicate a change in topic in the article, where the writer is moving in a new direction, and so serve as signposts to orient the reader.

As discussed in the previous chapter, boxed text and panels help to distinguish information and are incredibly important to a lot of magazine design. Alongside bullet points and indented text, these are some of the most common ways to lay out body copy so that it is not too uniform and dull.

For all these devices and other font styles (such as the use of bold or italics), the important point is that body copy, the substantial portion of text in the article, stands as the baseline from which text can be organised visually. There should be uniformity across body copy in a magazine – not simply on the page, but also between articles – that emphasises professional design.

Too much uniformity, however, makes a publication look dull. The use of different font styles for such things as headings, subheadings and standfirsts, as well as textual devices such as boxouts, drop letters and tables, creates a dynamic rather than static design. When reading a novel, we will concentrate on a narrative for an extended period of time, but this is not how we read a

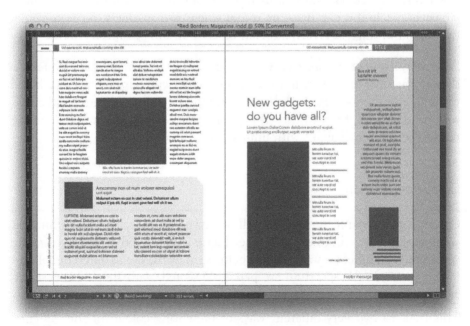

Figure 5.2 Elements such as boxouts and captions help text stand out

magazine: instead, our eyes move about the pages, taking in snippets of inform-ation before returning to concentrate on the articles that appear to be of most interest.

Colour

Like typography, colour is another subject that could easily be dealt with in an entire book and will only be dealt with here fairly briefly in terms of preparing the reader to start thinking of design.

Today there are very few national magazines that are not printed in full colour throughout, although this is a relatively recent phenomenon having only really become predominant since the rise of the glossies in the 1970s. And yet the impact of colour is so important, drawing the reader into the page, that we tend to consider magazines printed in monochrome as being less vivid. Certainly advertisers do not like black and white, which is one reason why so many magazines are printed in colour.

Ironically, because colour print is so prevalent in the magazine world, there are times when use of monochrome can have a significant effect: black and white, as many photographers know, often picks up gradations of tone much more effectively than colour and so is used to give an 'arty' appeal to some features. However, while this can have an appeal when used sparingly, no commercial title would willingly revert to monochrome for all its pages.

Alternatively, publications that wish to emphasise their more radical creden-tials, or their independence from advertisers, may willingly embrace black and white to give themselves a feel that is closer to a fanzine or underground publi-cation. In general, though, those magazines that are printed in monochrome tend to be very small affairs with limited budgets for design.

Colour perception

Colour is perceived in the eye via cells called cones that distinguish different combinations of red, green and blue. Light is part of the electromagnetic spectrum, with different wavelengths being seen by the eye as different colours: longer waves in the spectrum are perceived as red, with shorter waves seen as blue.

This leads to two very different ways of presenting colour for the designer. The first is via a computer screen, where pixels display the primary hues red, green or blue light, mixing them with surrounding pixels to create any of a potential 16.7 million colours. This creates what is known as the RGB (red, green, blue) model of colour perception, and mixing all the primary colours together equally gives white light.

Print, however, works by colour *reflection*. Some of the wavelengths in a spectrum are absorbed when they hit a surface, while others are reflected back. In print, the combination of colours works best when the secondary, rather than primary, hues are mixed – that is cyan, magenta and yellow (CMY). These are the hues for inks (as opposed to paints) that are obtained when blue and green are mixed to give cyan, red and blue are mixed to give magenta, and red and green are mixed to give yellow.

Mixing all colours equally should give black, but in practice this tends to result in a muddy, brownish colour. For this reason, black is added to the mix to give what is referred to as the CMYK ('K' from blacK) model of colour perception.

In addition to mixing inks, colour is affected by another range of values known as hue, saturation and value. Hue refers to the colour itself, and saturation is the amount of that hue present on the page (for example, a darker or lighter red): 100 per cent is complete colour, 0 per cent no colour (in print, this is grey rather than white). Value represents the relative brightness of a colour: at 100 per cent it becomes white, at 0 it becomes black.

Colour separation

Because of the way colour works on the page, by absorbing certain wavelengths and reflecting others, print has evolved over the past two centuries in particular to enable colours to be represented as accurately as possible.

When an image is imported into a computer program, either through scanning or from a digital camera, it will appear on the screen in an RGB format, that is each shade of colour is formed by merging the hues red, green and blue. However, as we have already seen, this is no good for print, which is why certain programs such as Adobe Photoshop allow you to separate out the colours and convert them to a format suitable for printing.

Colour separation works out the colour channels for cyan, magenta, yellow and black (and an advanced image editor such as Photoshop allows you to view each of these channels separately). This results in four separate images, each of which can be fed through a different coloured part of the press to build up a full-colour picture.

Ink is transparent, and the process of printing with ink has often been called 'mixing light', in that unlike pigments such as paint it is still possible to see the colour underneath, whereas paint covers all the layers beneath it. In practice, the yellow plate is printed first, and to this is added cyan (which when mixed with different amounts of yellow produces greens) and then red to build up all other colours. Where there is no ink on the page, the paper will show through as white, and black is added finally to emphasise dark shades or for text.

The CMYK system of printing is also known as process colour. For designers, this can create problems in that colours as they appear on screen may be subtly different to those in print, and colour calibration of monitors can be quite a time-consuming process. Even then, an art editor never completely knows how a colour will appear on the page until it is printed, hence the development of such things as 'cromies', or colour proofs, that will be discussed in the next chapter.

Another colour system that has been devised is the Pantone colour system – a system of shades whereby every colour is given a number that corresponds to a certain hue, saturation and value. By entering a Pantone number, the print system picks the exact colour from an internationally agreed set of hues – although there will always be slight vagaries from magazine to magazine due to such things as variances in paper quality.

Psychology and symbolism

Colour has an important psychological and cultural effect on us, so that we have learnt to associate certain values with different colours. Blue, for example, is typically seen as calming, red as either warming or aggressive depending on its context.

Whether these responses to colour are 'hard-wired' as it were into our psyches or more the result of cultural and social values is beyond the scope of this book. Art editors should probably beware of relying too much on the former, however, particularly if they have to work for an international audience. In Japan, for example, the same word is used to denote green and blue, and while white is a colour associated with marriage in the west, for Japanese people it is the colour worn to funerals.

This brings us on to the clearly social elements of colour, where they fulfil a particular symbolism such as indicating rank or political affiliation. Some colours may be used in different cultures to indicate a particular festival or year, and so articles dealing with these topics may subtly reinforce an approach or angle by using related hues.

Branding

While colour symbolism is important within a magazine for certain associations, such as red, white and blue for a story on the USA or Union Jack, colour can also have an added significance for magazines in terms of branding. Advertisers have for a long time worked on building up certain associations between colours and products, for example orange with a mobile phone company of the same name, or red and Coca-Cola. Colour branding often developed as a way to circumvent other advertising restrictions for particular goods, so that the manufacturers of Silk Cut cigarettes hoped that when anyone saw a particular shade of purple, they would immediately think of their cigarettes.

Such branding associations are often employed by magazine designers to promote their title. It is rare for branding to work by colour alone – there are simply too many magazines with red somewhere in the title for this to work – but in combination with a particular logo or typeface colour is an effective tool in creating a brand.

Photography

Ever since it was introduced in the early twentieth century, photography has become an essential ingredient in what we expect from magazines. Indeed, throughout the last hundred years it is in magazine titles that the most innovative and experimental designs combining word and image have often appeared.

While the considerations of what makes a good photo are beyond the scope of this title, the importance of photography and how to use an image are essential to magazine production.

Larger magazines will employ photographers (either working solely for that title or employed by a publishing company to work across multiple titles), but many rely on freelances. The other sources for photos are picture libraries and PR companies. The latter can be useful for such things as studio shots of individuals or products that may be covered by the magazine, but they will also seek to pressurise an editor to include rather dull images of a particular person or item that they wish to promote – and which may not be part of a good story.

When using photography, being dull is probably one of the worst charges that can be laid against an image. Indeed, for many magazines, varying photographs with other forms of illustration is a good way to prevent pages looking too uniform. Photos themselves should be used to illustrate quickly what an article is about. This may emphasise any emotional impact that emerges from a story, or allow the reader to identify with any people who feature in it. On a more mundane level, they may simply identify what is being discussed, although articles that rely on a product shot or portrait as the main illustration run the danger of providing rather boring layouts.

Unlike newspaper photography, however, the sheer variety of magazines means that it can be difficult to make overall suggestions that will fit every type of publication. What is important is to understand the audience: the rather graphic and extreme images that appear in *Bizarre* magazine, for example, will never go down well with the readers of *Homes and Gardens*.

This said, the importance of illustration and making a point cannot be underestimated. If readers can see a scene or item – for example, a new building or a car – it will help them understand the significance of an article in a way that verbal description alone simply cannot achieve.

Beyond this, photographs set the emotional response to a feature and, it must be said, they have learnt a great deal in this regard from advertising. While this may not be considered such a good thing by those used to working on newspapers or cultural critics of the magazine industry, the appeal of the glossies is precisely because they embody many of the desires and aspirations of their readers in a vivid format.

Types of photograph

The kinds of images that tend to appear in magazines largely fall into one of a number of categories: portraits, action shots, scenes or product shots.

Portraits, which may be head shots or full-length images of a subject, are a staple of nearly every type of magazine, and serve a number of important functions. The most obvious is that they immediately identify the subject being written about: if we have a photograph of a mountain climber or movie star, then we know who is under discussion and will recognise that person if they are a celebrity. For all photographs commissioned by a magazine, the photographer will need to get the subject to sign a model-release form, allowing the image to be used in the publication.

The issue of celebrity raises another feature regarding the use of such images. Glamorous shots of famous people have long been a way of enabling (or, depending on your point of view, seducing) readers to identify with particular desires and aspirations and have often been used by advertisers to sell products and editors to sell magazines. More recently, celebrity photography in titles such as *Heat* has tended not towards the sycophantic but rather towards the gossipy and bitchy, taking a lead from tabloid newspapers to use paparazzi photos that portray individuals in a less than glamorous light.

Figure 5.3 Magazines such as *National Geographic* are rightly famous for their photography. Image courtesy of Flip Nicklin/National Geographic Creative.

While faces and bodies sell – sometimes to the dismay of critics who lay much of the blame for the dissatisfaction that many females feel around their own bodies at the door of magazine editors – the preponderance of portraits means that they have lost their impact. Scenes offer great scope to an art designer: a dramatic landscape, or lovingly arranged home interior, can provide a stunning backdrop to a feature that will draw in the reader's attention. A title such as *National Geographic* has become famous for the quality of photographs that it uses to present the world around us. And this is an important point about such images: they are not merely decoration but often provide useful inform-ation that cannot be conveyed by words alone. Even B2B titles may find that photographs of a factory or industrial setting can immediately present the reader with a sense of what is going on in a story.

The images that are most fun to do, but also the most difficult to achieve, are action shots. Sport titles, for example, require images that capture a game during the thick of things to give an impression of what happened and the atmosphere of a sporting event. Many other titles, such as automobile magazines, will try to add some drama to their images by conveying speed and movement in a single image rather than a static shot.

Which leads finally on to product photography: often under-rated, there is a real skill to creating vibrant images of inanimate objects, which in the hands of a skilful photographer often borders on fetishism. Food magazines, for example, will expend a great deal of time and attention on making the food look as desirable as possible – even to the extent of employing plenty of artificial ingredients and props.

Shape and position

Just as variety in magazines comes from alternating photographs and other forms of illustration, so DTP software has made it easier than ever to experiment with the way that images are arranged on the page. It is much more common in magazines than newspapers to present photos in a dynamic fashion where images will be at angles or dominate much more of the page than would be given over to print in a paper.

Dramatic images can serve as the focal point for an introduction, taking up a page or the entirety of a DPS, with a standfirst appearing over the photograph. Alternatively, one useful approach is to use the image to break up the page, so that a small part is given over to white space and text while the rest is covered with a large, vivid photo.

Figure 5.4 Experiment with position, shape and cropping of an image

Long, vertical pictures can have an unusual effect because we are so used to seeing images in landscape mode (which fits the way our peripheral vision works to 180 degrees in either direction). Including such an image in a feature immediately forces the reader's eyes to move up and down the page, enabling the designer to build and control such motion across a feature.

When including images, square images tend to be the dullest; rectangles are less symmetrical, and so attract attention to the page, and it is very common for tabloid-style magazines to employ a larger number of shapes (such as stars for celebrities) to create more visual impact. Even regular shapes, however, become much more interesting when laid out as a photomontage; for example, different locations in a city used as a mosaic in a travel feature. Such images become a sort of visual box or panel, with short captions providing important information to the reader in a fashion that can be taken in immediately.

In addition to considering where to place a photo, and what shape it should take, cropping an image can add greatly to its impact: the important detail needs to be framed in the picture. When taking photos, the photographer will spend a lot of time considering how the subject is framed, but it is not always possible, particularly on location, to get the perfect image. An editor or layout artist may take a photograph and simply use one part of it to create a stronger impression.

Zooming in on a subject is one way to add drama or excitement to an image, creating an unusual angle that can add suspense and tension. Too much, of course, and the image becomes unrecognisable, but it can also be necessary simply to remove redundant detail (such as additional figures who are not essential to the story).

Ethical considerations

The ability to adjust pictures to improve quality raises a number of questions about the ease with which digital manipulation of photographs can have ethical consequences.

Magazines, like newspapers, are often faced with the temptation to make the image say what they want it to say. In 2006, the CBS publicity magazine *Watch* included a photograph of one of its news anchors, Katie Couric, in which her neck and waistline had been raised to make her look thinner – a practice that is common for images included in fashion or men's magazines, but caused concern when applied to a picture for a serious publication.

But image manipulation predates digital technologies (which simply make the process easier). In 1989, *Time* magazine had a front-cover image of Oprah Winfrey in which her head was spliced onto the body of another actress. The publication got into more trouble with its 1994 cover featuring O.J. Simpson, which was manipulated (digitally this time) to make the actor on trial for murder appear more menacing, according to critics.

The issue is less whether images are altered in themselves – this will happen to a lesser or greater degree with nearly all cover photographs, for example – than what the intended consequences are. Even without manipulation, an image may be used in such a way as to distort the truth, and this is the real ethical consideration.

When a photo is taken, the photographer selects what he or she considers most important about that scene. Likewise, when the image is cropped and framed in a magazine, that, in turn, may transform the reader's perception of an event. Images used for such things as publicity, celebrity or fashion are always going to be viewed differently to those that have a photojournalistic intention, which purport to document what has been going on at a specific time or place.

In addition, there are certain other considerations when using photos of individuals. Some of these, such as copyright, will be considered in Chapter 7, but it is worth bearing in mind some of the guidelines of IPSO with regard to taking and using photographs. For example, it is unacceptable to photograph individuals in private places without their consent, and to continue photographing people when asked to stop can constitute harassment.

The most serious concerns, however, are around photographing children. Without even going into the murky waters of taste and decency (which have affected teen magazines at times in particular), no child under 16 should be photographed or interviewed without the consent of appropriate guardians or authorities (such as a school).

Illustrations and graphics

While most of this chapter has concentrated on photography for magazines, alternative forms of illustration should never be forgotten. As well as larger illustrations to accompany features, graphical elements are part of the branding that runs throughout a magazine.

As well as simply illustrating an article, graphic communication is intended to help a reader receive information as quickly as possible. Sometimes this works with very small elements that appear apparently incidentally on a page, such as a star-rating system with reviews that can convey at a glance what the reviewer thought of a topic. Elements such as icons or logos, may also help to orientate a reader in a magazine, guiding them through the navigation of different sections. Furthermore, graphics emphasise the corporate brand of the magazine, using logos and typography to emphasise that the title is a coherent entity.

When employing illustrators, some of this graphics work may be done in-house by the same artists who engage in layout, or freelances might be hired for a specific task. In contrast to photography, where there is usually some direct visual connection with the subject written about on the same pages, a drawing or piece of artwork offers the opportunity for a more abstract link to be made. This is not a strength of British consumer magazines today, although there are some better examples in the B2B sector where editors sometimes seek to spice up their copy with more interesting illustrations.

Although there are plenty of designers who will still draw their compositions by hand, the majority today will use computer applications such as Adobe Illustrator and Photoshop to produce their work. This has the added advantage of not requiring scanning at a later date and so can be delivered by disk or email to an art editor.

DTP

DTP, or desktop publishing, is essential to modern magazine design. While occasionally a title will use traditional composition methods, these really have no place any more in the professional publishing world and DTP is a fundamental skill for many people working with magazines. When titles need to employ a layout artist, they will hire designers as the best suited to the job, but it is increasingly important for even editors and other journalists to know their way around a DTP package; for those starting out in a publishing career, it can be very useful when landing a subbing job or making amendments to a feature.

DTP, the skills involved in laying out designs using a computer, can encompass more than paper-based publications such as magazines, newspapers or books, to incorporate web sites, retail packaging and promotional items. It began in 1985 when Aldus (later to merge with Adobe) released PageMaker for the Apple Mac, the first software program to allow WYSIWYG (what you see is what you get) layout on screen.

Early software was very primitive by today's standards, but new technology was increasingly being used in newsrooms by the end of the 1980s and saw a real boom in the 1990s as computer prices dropped and more and more companies saw the virtue of streamlining design.

Although often associated with graphic design, the latter refers more to the creative process of coming up with ideas for presentation, whereas DTP is more concerned with the mechanical process of laying out those ideas. For magazines, it brings together the elements of text, image and colour considered in the previous chapter.

From QuarkXPress to Adobe InDesign

Although not the first DTP package to be released, throughout the 1990s and early 2000s magazine design was dominated by QuarkXPress. The program was launched in 1987 for the Apple Macintosh, followed by a version for Windows in 1992 that was largely neglected until the early 2000s.

Part of the early success of Quark lay in the fact that it could be modified to include additional features via a system known as XTensions, but more than anything else it combined a simple interface with reliability. However, the fact that it had gained a 90 per cent market share by the end of the 1990s, its very high price and slow development times led to charges that it had become a monopoly. In 1999, Adobe released InDesign as a direct competitor to Quark.

Although substantially cheaper, InDesign initially did not particularly appeal to designers. This changed with the release of InDesign 2.0, launched at the same time as QuarkXPress 5.5 in 2002: while Adobe's program supported Apple's new MacOS X, Quark did not. More significantly, InDesign included support for Portable Document Format (PDF) as standard, which had begun to transform the way that magazines and other documents were prepared for press.

In the past decade, Adobe has continually improved InDesign, as well as integrating it very closely with the other designer favourite, Photoshop. Although its move from the Creative Suite to a subscription-based model, Creative Cloud, was contentious, the fact that this allows designers to continually keep abreast of new developments has firmly established InDesign as the leading software for publishing.

Using the grid

Central to most modern magazine design is the grid – which has become almost synonymous with the professional approach. The purpose of the grid is to provide a basic template that will enable consistency across the magazine. If every page starts from scratch, although individually this could result in fabulous and exciting designs, the overall effect for the magazine would be to make it look much more amateurish.

The grid becomes the outline on which can be laid all other elements of the page – the title, columns and images, as well as any boxouts or other components. Certain features, such as page numbers or a magazine logo, will always appear in the same place so that the reader can navigate through pages easily, but others, such as images, will be laid out in different positions so that there is also some variety. The point of the grid is to provide a bedrock for the rest of magazine design, not to enforce dull and sterile conformity across every page.

Ideally, the grid should correspond to some kind of ratio, dividing the page in halves, thirds or quarters. It will establish column positions and also gutters between those columns and a margin around the edge of the page. A slightly more complex but commonly employed grid is to divide the page by the ratio of 1:1.414, which corresponds to the ratio of the width of an A4 page to its length. This divides the page into four equal quarters, which can then be further divided into equal sections using the same ratio.

As the basis for creative and professional design, the grid will provide a series of lines on the page that can be used effectively for variety within proportion. For example, a very commonly employed grid divides the page into 12 columns,

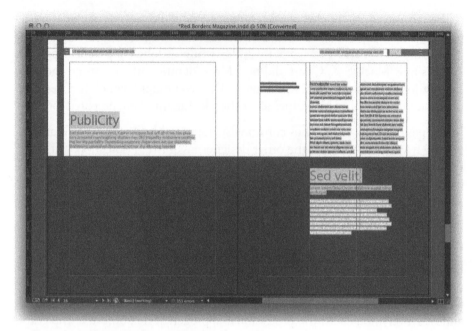

Figure 5.5 Designing with the grid

though no magazine will ever print 12 columns of text – you would be lucky to get more than a couple of words to each line. However, what this basic grid does is enable the designer to set one page out with two columns, another with three and yet another with four – an easy way to distinguish a lead-in page from other articles, or from news stories. While the column widths will vary from story to story, they will still remain in proportion to each other as long as they follow the grid.

Once a grid is in place, items should be aligned to the guidelines consistently: if items hang over grid lines or move from place to place for no reason, this will fail to create a harmonious impression across a magazine. Actually, good designers will sometimes 'jump the grid', staggering a page element across the page in an unexpected manner – but they know why they want to do this because they are used to creating pages that demonstrate variety within a consistent framework.

Master pages and templates

DTP packages allow designers to create master pages. These are not printed out, but once a grid and overall style is determined, these contain information that will be used in the rest of the magazine. There will be a master page for the left-hand and right-hand pages of the publication, each of which contains placeholders for such things as page numbers, logos and other material that typically goes into the header and footer of a page.

Templates are the next step up from a master page, and a title will probably use several of these for different types of article or different sections of a magazine. Rather than designing each page from scratch, the layout artist will open a template and begin to drop copy and photos onto the screen – this allows him or her to experiment with the presentation while maintaining overall consistency with other pages.

The template will contain the grid with specified columns, and may have sample holders for text, headings and illustrations. For example, it might be the house style always to begin with an image in the top right- or left-hand corner of a page, and headings will probably appear in the same spot so that they do not jump up and down from feature to feature.

The problem with this approach is that while it makes a publication look much smoother and professional, it can also result in pages looking very similar and thus a little dull. The task for a good designer is to make proper use of a template to prevent a magazine looking as though it was thrown together in a chaotic

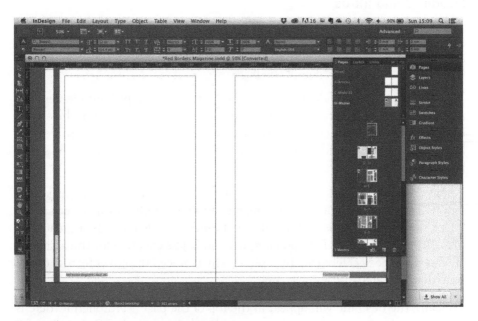

Figure 5.6 A master page in InDesign

fashion, but templates should also serve as a launch pad for experimenting with different areas of design.

Style sheets

Along with templates, style sheets are another tool within DTP packages that can help to speed up design. Style sheets are used to provide default settings for text in headers, standfirsts, body copy, paragraphs and so on.

For example, you may decide that the standard font for body copy in features is 9 point Garamond on a 9.5 point body and with a 3 point space at the beginning of paragraphs. Likewise, subheadings may be 10 point Helvetica on an 11 point body in a different hue to the rest of the text. These elements can be entered into the style palette in Quark or InDesign and saved; when a designer wishes to create a subheading or paragraph of body text, he or she simply selects one of those entries so that formatting is applied automatically and quickly.

As with templates, style sheets will be set up early in the life of a magazine and not tinkered with too much unless the publication undergoes a substantial redesign.

Headings and intros

The previous chapter discussed the use of typography as a visual element on a page, but it is also important to discuss how titles and standfirsts work as building blocks in the design of the page.

The headline is, alongside any large images, the most important element for attracting the reader's attention. It has to convey information about the article in a very limited number of words and, unsurprisingly, must be considerably larger than the surrounding text to draw in the reader's eye as he or she is leafing through a publication.

Verbally, of course, titles must be appropriate to the audience of the magazine: serious and sober publications may appreciate some subtle wordplay, but while 'Meet the shadow minister for militant Islam' immediately has a great deal to say for the readers of The Spectator, it is much less effective for the audience of Nuts than 'Sexy celebs caught topless', which graced the cover feature of the issue that appeared at the same time.

Typically, the headline will appear at the top of the page – although if there is a strong graphic image it may appear immediately beneath this. Sometimes, for variety, a magazine will try running the headline through or alongside body copy – but this is nearly always confusing for the reader. What can be more successful, however, is to place the main headline beneath a standfirst; while this is not as logical to read as following on with the intro, it can make for a bold design if used relatively sparingly.

In magazines (in contrast to some parts of newspapers), headlines outside the news pages at least tend to run across columns and only be one or two lines deep. Usually the headline is in a different colour from the main body copy – indeed, should be in a different colour to make it stand out as the reader glances from page to page. While there is no hard and fast rule as to whether a headline should be sans serif or not, it is certainly the case that it will often be bolder to help emphasise the words.

The shape of the headline, as well as the standfirst or intro, is important, in giving balance to a page. Standfirsts are usually presented as blocks of text that work as a graphical object in their own right, adding a dash of colour and visual interest to a page. As well as standing out visually, they also present concise information that will expand on the title and present the reader with key features that will help him or her decide whether to continue reading.

Mechanical specifications: margins, bleed and trim size

When laying out pages, the columns and graphics that go into most articles will need to have a margin around the page. Unlike newspapers, however, where this margin is designed to allow some leeway when printing at high speeds, margins are added to magazine pages for aesthetic effect. White space around the edge of text and between columns makes text easier to read.

For some pages, however, particularly those with a background colour or illustrations that run over the entire spread or just part of it, ink will need to go right up to the edge of the page for the best effect. This is referred to as 'bleed', and means that in a design program such as Quark or InDesign, colour is taken over the actual edge of the page, typically to a distance of 5 mm or so beyond the trim marks.

Printers are able to cope with this because printing takes place on pieces of paper that are larger than the final page size of the magazine (usually 20 mm larger on each side). Trim size refers to the actual dimensions of this final page, which gives the canvas for designers and layout artists to work with. Crop marks, or small crossed lines, are placed at the corners of the page to indicate where the page should be trimmed.

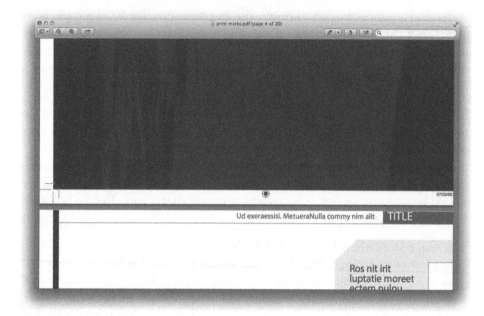

Figure 5.7 Bleed and trim marks on a layout

Finally, the other mechanical specification that can affect the way pages are laid out is gutter width. This is the fold where pages meet, and varies according to the type of binding that is used to hold the magazine together, whether it is perfect binding (glue) or saddle stitched with staples. In different parts of a magazine, particularly larger publications that are perfect bound, some pages will look further apart and so the gutter width will need to be changed to take this into account. Unless you are creating a DPS with an image that runs across both pages, no content should go into the gutter as it will generally be unreadable.

Proofing

Proofing is often closely tied to the subbing process outlined in Chapter 4, whereby an editor will proofread articles to check for accuracy and consistency. Indeed, the terms are often used synonymously, but here the term proofing (as opposed to proofreading) means checking the final layout of pages for such things as colour accuracy.

A printer will want some type of guarantee from the publisher that the files delivered to them for printing will be as accurate as possible. Any changes made after delivery will incur extra costs, and the printer also wishes to determine that any mistakes on the final page are (barring failures in the mechanical process such as misaligned plates) the responsibility of the publisher.

This is why proofing the final artwork is so important. Much of the pre-press work that had to be done manually in previous years is now handled as part of the PDF process, which is one reason why InDesign became a market leader. Nonetheless, art editors will still need to visually check all pages before they are sent off to the printer.

It is worth bearing in mind the limitations of proofs: because of possible small variations in inks and papers used during the printing process, pages cannot always look exactly the same. These variations can exist even between the same types of press (though to a much lesser degree), but most proofs will be produced on a different system. Nonetheless, proofing is still extremely important to minimise unpleasant surprises before printing begins.

The cover

As already discussed in Chapter 3, the cover is the most important element for selling a magazine on the newsstand. While the building blocks that go into a successful cover for different magazines operating in diverse markets would take too much space to describe in detail here, there are common features that do work across nearly all of them.

- An eye-catching photograph or illustration: rather than a montage, this nearly always consists of an A4 size image that covers most, if not all, of the front cover, and is appropriate for the audience under consideration. As noted before, consumer magazines in particular tend to be very similar (and thus rather conservative) in their choice of cover models so that – by image alone – it can be very difficult to distinguish one title from another.
- Cover lines: these are extremely important in making readers pick up a title, and so need to be short (so that they do not crowd out the main image) but punchy, conveying the meaning of an article concisely. Some titles may include page numbers, but better practice is to offer an innovative cover title that leads the reader on to the contents page where they will look up the story while browsing. Once they have it in their hands, they are more likely to purchase the magazine.

   There has been some debate about the significance of differences between cover lines and actual story titles. It is not uncommon for the two not to match up precisely – the words that appear on a cover may be fewer words in larger print to grab the reader's attention. Too much variance, however, and this can be frustrating in that the reader may not know where the article appears inside the magazine.

- Title: the title of a magazine serves an important function as a logo, branding the magazine. Its position, nearly always in the top quarter of a front cover, also serves a practical purpose. When publications are stacked one on top of the other in a newsagent or supermarket, this will be the only part of the magazine that can be seen clearly by a prospective buyer. As such, bright bold colours and clear typography that can be read from a distance are essential.

A cover, then, is a combination of image and type – an image on its own, however striking, is unlikely to say anything to the reader. Cover lines provide a context for the picture, one that should intrigue a person standing at the newsstand and, ideally, provide an unusual angle on topics they are already interested in.

Because it is so important in selling the magazine, the cover – combining all the elements of colour, image and typography discussed in this chapter, as well as principles of design that are the subject of the next chapter – is usually designed (or at least overseen) by the art editor. While other factors such as seasonal variations and poor weather or economic conditions affect sales to a lesser or greater degree, a poor cover is one of the biggest mistakes that an editorial and art department can make.

6
Designing for digital

Over the past decade, magazines have fully embraced the digital sphere, although the explosion of mobile devices in the past five years still presents challenges that publishers are sometimes struggling to deal with. At the very least, magazines will have an accompanying web site which is also much more, now, than a simple advertisement for a print title.

Mobile, however, has resulted in brands often having to rethink how they create their titles. As we have seen in Chapter 1, the huge increase in tablets and smartphones is one of the reasons why print publications are less appealing than previously. Smartphones themselves initially seemed less of a threat – or opportunity. The smaller screens of such devices was such that they offered little comparison to the carefully designed layouts that magazines had been developing for a century or more, but as phones have increased in size and, for many people, replaced desktop and laptop computers as well as tablets as their primary computing device, so they have become an important part of the mix.

To begin with, a number of publishers tended to simply port PDFs of their titles straight to mobile, which can often be a frustrating experience for readers. As such, in this chapter I shall consider some of the different options that brands need to consider when producing for the web and mobile devices.

Such challenges and opportunities are indicated by a recent comment by Nicholas Thompson, editor of NewYorker.com: 'For a long time, the website was a place where the magazine's stories were supposed to be presented and read in a digital format. But it wasn't a place with its own particularly high ambitions.' This was true for a great many magazines other than *The New Yorker*, but on that title at least the ambitions have vastly expanded since Thompson joined in 2010, growing the digital audience to more than 10 million across the web and mobile platforms, with a catalogue of blogs, apps and original video as well as an active social media presence.

Web publishing

As Thompson observes, for a long time *The New Yorker*'s digital strategy consisted of a web site and . . . a web site. Obviously digital audiences comprise much more than visitors to such a site, but it often remains at the heart of any digital strategy. For that particular title, the overall strategy is, ultimately, to convert as many visitors into print subscribers as that remains the core activity of the brand. For many other magazines, however, online-first may be turning into an online-only strategy – certainly for a raft of recent titles such as *Good* (magazine.good.is) or *Jezebel* (jezebel.com) which have only ever existed in digital form.

When creating a digital magazine, many of the elements considered in the previous chapter – such as writing good editorial or producing compelling photographs – remain the same, but if a magazine web site is to be more than just shovelware for the print edition, then several other factors should be taken into account:

- Original content: in the earliest of days for magazine brands, the web was – at best – a repository of content that was previously found in the print version. If anything, such was the entirely reasonable concern of publishers that giving away content for free online would lose them revenue, most web sites were a much-reduced version of the print title. By contrast today, the very best titles will regularly produce new content that does not make it into print, taking advantage of the much cheaper production costs of the web to expand their audience through new stories posted on a daily basis.

- Blogs: one of the big opportunities offered by online platforms is blogging, which is now widely recognised as something of a genre in its own right, less formal and often more immediate than standard articles or news packages. Blogging is an ideal way to offer comment and analysis on events crucial to readers' concerns, where journalists can develop their own voices to appeal to readers.

- Multimedia: multimedia, in the form of audio podcasts or video for a web site, has often been one of the biggest challenges to publishers because, in contrast to more traditional broadcasters, it has been very alien to the way they have done business before. Until recently, proper equipment and expertise to produce good-quality audio-visual material was also expensive. While it can remain a significant cost, recent trends (not least the rise of mo-jo, or mobile journalism) have reduced this greatly. Now it is increasingly part of the workflow, something to be factored in before an article begins rather than something that is tacked on at the end of the process.

- Community and social media: while magazine brands have always taken, rightly, a pride in their position as niche media that can bring together interested parties who need to know about a particular issue, the ability of the internet to connect different people operates on a scale never seen before. As already remarked in Chapter 2, social media should be much more than a means to simply direct people to original articles, but rather is part of the conversation that stimulates readers' interests and, in turn, invites them to participate in the discussion through comments on articles and lively debate.
- Data and traffic: another major change in the way that publishers view digital offerings is the sheer wealth of data that web sites generate in terms of visitors and their habits (leaving aside, for a moment, the extremely rich information willingly submitted by people to social media sites which tends to be owned and used by those sites alone). Services such as Google Analytics are regularly used by publishers (along with log files stored on their own servers as well as a few alternatives) to digest who is looking at what and for how long. While this can tend to result in a lowest-common denominator – determining the value of web pages simply through counting the number of visitors – in other respects it is a valuable addition to the practice of auditing print copies that can help determine which content works best for readers and advertisers.

Figure 6.1 Social media has become an important part of the mix for magazines

The role of the online editor

For publications that have a serious web presence, an online editor may have as many responsibilities as the print editor. He or she will be expected to liaise with the publisher and sales team, as well as oversee editorial and graphic design departments. For smaller concerns, the print editor may also take charge of the web site, and in any case it is most likely that the online editor will report to the main magazine editor.

Here I shall concentrate on those elements that will probably be different to the role of a print editor, while noting that many of the tasks and responsibilities pointed out in Chapters 4 and 5 concerning editorial, art and production will also apply.

One significant difference is in terms of deadlines and the timescale of a web site. A web site in some ways is closer to a newspaper than a magazine in that visitors will expect to see content updated on a daily basis. Indeed, daily updates may not be enough, with journalists expected to contribute throughout the day as and when news becomes available, making an online publication more like a broadcast newsroom.

Once the technical infrastructure is in place (a server capable of dealing with thousands of page hits and shifting megabytes, or even gigabytes of data per hour), publishing to the web is much simpler than sending to print, although the cost of constant technical support and maintenance should not be under-estimated. In recent years, the fundamental principles of good web design have separated content (such as words and images or video) from the structure of a web site, how content is presented in a particular format to the end user, and its design, the look and feel of a page.

Professional web sites will now be dynamic, information stored in one or more databases that can be accessed by different types of page for different platforms, which is why separating structure and design from content is so important. If your reader is accessing a page from a mobile phone or digital television, their experience will be very different to that of someone who views the same information on a PC.

While many sites appear to have hundreds or even thousands of pages of content, in terms of design there will only be a few templates that strip out information from a database and present it to the reader. The virtue of this approach is that it makes it incredibly easy to redesign the whole site. In addition, it means that writers can concentrate on what they are good at – writing – entering their text into some form of content-management system and leaving final presentation of their content in the more capable hands of the designer who set up the original system.

In addition to overseeing the production cycle, then, which will result in content being uploaded on a daily basis for some sections, less often for others, the online editor will also have to consider ways to interact with readers on site. Interaction is key to what is often referred to as 'sticky' content, and increasingly web sites are becoming reliant on their visitors providing them with much of the original material that they use.

As well as taking responsibility for web production, the online editor will also probably have an overview of the brand's social media strategy (though for larger titles this may be split off and even be part of a marketing role). Individual journalists will tend to be active on social media sites such as Facebook and Twitter, but as an important function of such activity is often driving traffic to a site there also needs to be a co-ordinating strategy for the magazine as a whole, not simply publishing links to new stories but also engaging in conversations with the brand's readers.

Digital issues for mobile devices tend to fall into the remit of the art and production department, especially as some of the tools I shall be looking at later in this chapter tend to work as plug-ins for software such as InDesign.

Creating a web site

The possibilities for publishing on the web can be extremely complex, far more so than part of a single chapter can cover. In the two and a half decades since Tim Berners-Lee invented the World Wide Web, a wealth of software has become available that greatly simplifies that task, and I shall consider some of the best applications to begin publishing online.

Of the various aspects that affect creating a digital magazine, the starting point is that it should be capable of handling multiple users, from readers or subscribers who might be able to leave comments on particular articles, to myriad writers and content providers uploading text and multimedia, as well as editors and production staff who will manage the workflow for going from copy to final publication. As such, pretty much every web site for such magazines will be a content-management system in some shape or form, whether a bespoke application built up from scratch or something off the shelf.

In addition, web design has itself gone through two revolutions in the twenty-first century. The first, so-called Web 2.0, has very much become part of the new standards for creating online sites since the term was coined by Tim O'Reilly in 2004. At its heart, Web 2.0 saw the process of such sites increasingly replacing desktop software as the point at which users performed various operations, with data being processed on a remote server before being delivered to their screens. Thus commonly used sites such as Google Maps or Facebook process huge amounts of information to simplify processes such as finding a location or shopping. In addition, the past decade has seen an explosion in user-generated content, with millions of people online uploading videos and photos to sites such as YouTube and Pinterest, publishing their own material through blog software such as WordPress, or editing articles on Wikipedia.

In effect, the principles of Web 2.0 (web sites as applications, user-generated content and simplicity of publishing online) can be taken for granted as built into the current web and, while the internet is constantly evolving, suggestions that the next step be called Web 3.0 have never really taken hold in the public imagination. Something that publishers will probably need to take into account, however, when publishing online, is the second revolution, the effects of which are still working their way through the internet: HTML5.

HTML is the underlying set of instructions that governs the way that content is displayed in a browser. The specification for HTML5 was only finalised at the end of 2014 and not all browsers are yet fully compatible with it. With new standards for visual styling via Cascading Style Sheets (CSS3), it represents the way forward for modern software, allowing designers to create working applications that also look good and that will, when necessary, degrade functions gracefully in older browsers. It also allows designers to do things that were previously impossible without plug-ins such as Adobe Flash or Silverlight, to play videos or games for example. For a magazine brand, however, probably the most important thing about HTML5 is that it has been built with mobile devices in mind, so that it no longer matters whether you are viewing content on a desktop or your phone: if your web site is created according to the HTML5 specification, it can be automatically set to display itself to its best advantage no matter what it is viewed on.

The main publishing platforms, such as WordPress (the software behind *The New Yorker*, *Techcrunch* and *Variety*) or Drupal (*Mother Jones*, *Popular Science*), are increasingly implementing HTML5 through templates and core improvements to the software. Of these two, WordPress – which began life as a blogging application – has shown itself remarkably apt when employed as a content-management system, and is the software I would recommend to anyone thinking of setting up a magazine online for the first time. It can be downloaded from wordpress.org and then installed on your own server (and most web hosts will automatically bundle in WordPress as part of their package, making installation little more than choosing a domain name and title for your site, an administrator name and password, then clicking install). Drupal is considerably more sophisticated and allows users finer control over their end product, but it likewise requires a great deal more expertise

Figure 6.2 WordPress is the software used to create many magazine web sites

to use and lacks the large user base that has created a host of plug-ins and add-ons for WordPress.

Blogs

While blogging emerged at the turn of the century as an easy – and almost entirely amateur – means for internet users to express themselves to a growing audience, in the past decade blogs have become established as a mainstay of professional web publishing. Even in the early 2000s, web visitors were beginning to turn to self-run blogs in categories such as sport and politics for authoritative insight that, previously, would have depended on newspapers, print magazines and broadcasters to see the light of day. Now, brands such as *National Geographic*, *Time Out* and *Cosmopolitan* run blogs on subjects as diverse as travel, events and sex and relationships.

Certainly modern blogs have far outgrown their humble origins as a web diary for individuals, although that tends to present a problem in terms of defining exactly what a blog is if its subject matter may incorporate anything. As such, here is a non-exhaustive list of some of the primary factors that make up a blog:

- Informality: in contrast to the main editorial of a professional publication in particular, a blog will usually have a more direct and even chatty tone.

That is actually harder than it seems: if a blog is to be seen as part of a brand, then it will still have to maintain some of the characteristics of that brand. Some of this is common sense – although blogs may invite greater freedom in terms of the voice that can be used, language that is grammatically incorrect or poorly spelt means that it will never be taken seriously. It should also deal with subjects and themes that are consonant with the magazine's main concerns; a blog is not an excuse to veer towards wildly personal (and irrelevant) tangents. At the same time, if a blog lacks any personal touch, especially for formal titles, then it may come across as weirdly corporate and robotic.

- Timeliness: online publishing has meant that many titles now need to publish material on a regular basis, rather than according to the monthly or weekly schedules that used to dominate print magazines. As such, there is something of a blurred boundary between blogging and main editorial, but certainly readers will expect to see regular updates to blogs that follow up themes across the year.

- Interactivity: again, online magazines may often feel that interactivity is something that is intrinsic to their web site, but in practice a major activity – leaving comments and feedbacks – is sometimes restricted to blogs. In part this is because of the greater informality of tone; in contrast to professional journalists, readers may display an extremely varied and sometimes utterly random range of interests and abilities, and comments against carefully crafted articles can be somewhat distracting if the subject is a serious one such as politics or news.

- Guest writers: because online is not as limited in terms of the amount of content it can produce, blogs are also an excellent forum to allow guest writers to try out their skills without having to conform too much to the demands of the main editorial office. Indeed, there are some sites such as *The Huffington Post* that have made a virtue of building up entire sections of content from contributing bloggers.

The distinction between blogging and mainstream editorial may be a blurred one for some publications such as *The Huffington Post*, but for a wide range of publishers they have become an important means to test the waters in terms of what readers want. Writers and editors may explore certain themes through blogs, and also publish quickly to the web with a greater degree of understanding that the material could be more speculative and tentative. At the same time, some personal bloggers have gained immense influence through regularly publishing on topics that they care about passionately, such as the team behind heyuguys.com (which started as a personal blog back in 2008 and now is a major magazine on the film industry in its own right), or Paul Staines, the man behind the somewhat infamous Guido Fawkes political blog (order-order.com).

For a period of time, the role of blogging and its relationship to more traditional publishing resulted in a heated argument that pitched journalists and bloggers against each other. Certainly, there are plenty of journalists who blog (and are expected to blog by their employers as part of their work), but the fact that anyone could set up a blog using sites such as WordPress, Blogger and Typepad was something that could undermine the professionalism of journalism. The training that most journalists go through is intended to establish particular approaches to the gathering of news especially, one which places a greater emphasis on objectivity and the gathering of factual information from reliable sources. By contrast, many (if not most) bloggers tend to rely more on third-party sources and will follow a more subjective approach to a topic.

With regard to news, blogging will probably remain inferior, but if journalism is interpreted more widely then it has a very valuable role to play. Indeed, some practices that originated in blogs – such as linking to references and updating live content – are now commonplace across all the media. With regard to such updates, a big difference is that a responsible magazine will inform the reader when content is modified, something that remains unusual on most blogs.

Multimedia

While blogging indicates the ways in which magazines can experiment with tone of voice and approaches to readers in editorial, what was at first the biggest challenge and is now the biggest opportunity is multimedia. Since 2005, when the first video was uploaded to YouTube, more and more readers expect to see such content on the web pages that they visit. Between 1991 and 2014, the number of web sites in the world grew from one to one billion; in 2013, YouTube users alone were uploading 72 hours of video content *every minute*, with one billion hours' worth of content being watched on the site every month.

For much of its history in the twentieth century, creating multimedia was an expensive and time-consuming process, requiring well-trained professionals working in studios with complex equipment. Now a huge number of people carry HD-quality video cameras in their pocket and are used to communicating regularly via Skype or similar programs.

One consequence of this is that video has become something increasingly mundane: I still remember a tech demo by a video card manufacturer in 1995 when the person demonstrating the new product became extremely excitable by the fact that it could process real time video (and, to be honest, I was also rather impressed by the postage-stamped stream that appeared on the monitor),

Figure 6.3 Sites such as that for the *NME* now regularly use video

but today if we can't see video on our phones we rightly assume that it is faulty in some way. That staple of science fiction, the video call, is very much part of everyday life.

Nonetheless, while viewers are perfectly content to watch shaky footage taken in poor lighting conditions, with no real thought given to such things as wind conditions, when speaking to friends and family, or coo over endless hours of extremely amateur cat and baby videos, they rightly expect much more from a professional brand. Creating video is much less expensive than before, and Apple in particular takes great pride in showcasing professional-looking video made with its iPhone, but taking a phone out of your pocket, pointing it at your subject, and hoping for the best is extremely unlikely to produce the best results. While a comprehensive guide to producing video for a site is beyond the remit of this book, here are some important considerations:

- Workflow: before even considering the technology involved, it's important to make sure that creating audio and video is part of your workflow.
  While multimedia was very much an afterthought for most magazines
  in the early days of the web, it is now firmly built into the process for the
  better brands. After all, just as no respectable publisher would take
  the attitude that it was acceptable to write copy and then leave design
  and layout till the very end, so any video that accompanies an article
  needs to be planned in advance. This means that videos should be scripted

and storyboarded, and while smaller titles may rely on staff to become multi-tasking in every way, for others multimedia production is handled by specialists, just as photography and layout would be.

- Camera: while a professional-level video camera will typically cost anywhere from £4,000 to £10,000 at the time of writing (with extremely high-end studio cameras costing much more), the best camera in the end is the one that you can use. For those multi-tasking staffers (or, indeed, users generating content for the web site), that may very well mean the camera in their phone. A major restriction of such devices, however, is the lens: one of the basic lessons for anyone interested in film school is to have three lenses – a 50mm one for regular shots, 24–35mm for moderate wide-angle shots and an 80–200mm lens for zooming. Likewise, the size of the aperture or f-number is important, often referred to as the 'speed' of the camera, in that it will allow more light in to prevent underexposed shots. (Counter-intuitively, the smaller the f-number, the larger the aperture, so a 50mm f/1.8 allows in more light than an f/4.) Smartphone cameras have greatly improved but the lens can be much more important than the amount of megapixels of data they can capture, which is why in practice many semi-professional video makers use digital SLR still cameras that can also capture video to flash cards and, more importantly, have interchangeable lenses.

- Lighting: while the lens is important for capturing light, the scene needs to be lit in the first place which can be a major problem indoors. A sure sign of amateur photography is a reliance on the flash (almost always in the worst place possible because if the subject is looking at the camera it will wash out their features and give them glaring red eyes). A typical set-up for illuminating a video scene is what is known as three-point lighting. The key light is the main and strongest source of light, with a fill light – softer than the main source – set at an angle across the main light to fill out the shadows (hence its name). Finally, there is a back light to separate the subject from the background; placed behind the subject, it helps them appear more three-dimensional.

- Audio: equally important to how your video looks is how it sounds. The best-lit scene with a high-end camera will still be amateurish if all viewers can hear is the sound of rushing wind. High-end cameras will often have an external microphone attached to them, but if you are going to be making a lot of video with lower-end equipment it is worth investing in decent microphones, to capture your audio, as well as such things as pop filters (which block the plosive sounds made when we pronounce certain words) and wind shields.

- Accessories: finally, there are various accessories that you can use to make your video look more professional. The most essential of these is a tripod, which will help deal with the issue of shake which can ruin footage. Even for those using a smartphone, a dedicated tripod is a must-have and, indeed, is probably the one thing alongside a decent external mic that will allow you to produce professional-looking video at minimal cost (after all, if you have someone willing to stand with a reflective surface in a relatively bright room, you can even get away without purchasing lights at a push). Less essential but frequently useful is the green screen: professional studios will have a room with green-coloured walls that can be removed (or chroma-keyed) during editing, but it is possible to get a decent effect with low-cost green fabric. During the editing process, software composites, that is layers, video streams together based on particular colours (chroma ranges). A colour in the top layer is rendered transparent so the underlying layer can be seen, and suddenly your subject's backdrop is no longer a cupboard off your main production room but the East Room of the White House.

Data and analytics

Another advantage of publishing online, especially for publishers hosting content on their own server, is that the simple activity of viewing web pages generates a huge amount of data that can be used to analyse trends for a brand. While it is clear to many publishers that their content has value, demonstrating that value as a return on investment (ROI) has often been difficult to achieve. In the days of print-only publications, they would commission reader surveys and focus groups to try and pin down what mattered most to their readers, but the constant traffic to web pages on a site stores up a huge amount of information that can help them decide what it is that readers want.

There are some very important caveats to this process, the most important of which is the difference between quantitative and qualitative analysis of content. The first, quantitative, is a way of measuring the value of content by counting definite and discrete units of information – how many web pages are visited on a site, how long users stay, if there are particular peak times for access and which countries readers come from, as well as what browser or devices they are using. Quantitative analysis has come on in leaps and bounds since the invention of the computer and spreadsheet, and unsurprisingly it is something that analytics software such as Google Analytics excels at.

Qualitative analysis, by contrast, is more concerned with underlying reasons and motivations for doing something – *why* a reader visits your web site in contrast to *what* they are doing once they open a page. Qualitative research seeks to uncover underlying trends and is best performed via interviews, focus groups and participation or observation; while computers can be helpful in terms of storing and presenting data, the actual research still works best when conducted by people.

As such, web analytics can be extremely useful for uncovering patterns of usage (that there is a spike of visitors at certain times of the day, week or month, whether readers are directed to your site from links or search engines, if they are using mobile devices to view content more than a desktop or notebook computer), but it does not provide a complete picture as to the value of a brand's content because it tells publishers nothing about why readers like that content. This has created a dangerous trend in recent years: because the information from site logs is so clear and apparently accurate to an almost unprecedented degree ('apparently' because some users may block certain information from being recorded), publishers have become fixated on such things as the volume of traffic to a site, sources and destinations and other, clearly quantitative data. What this cannot tell anyone is the reason why any individual clicked on a web site in the first place, or why they left. Many journalists complain, rightly, that this obsession with data results in a devaluing of their practice, reducing it to a number of hits and time spent on a page, information that can be of immense use when dealing with advertisers but which is much less useful when determining the significance of a particular article.

Nonetheless, web analytics remains an important tool for online publishers. Brands with access to their own server will be able to download logs that

Figure 6.4 Google Analytics is the most widely used software to track site traffic

calculate to the smallest degree information about any visits to that server, but in practice most will use a site such as Google Analytics (google.com/analytics) to strip out that data and present it in an easy to read format. Some alternatives include Piwik (piwik.org), Parse.ly (parsley.com) and KISSmetrics (kissmetrics. com), and though there are some differences between the interfaces of all of these, the fundamental task is the same: to track visitors and see what they are doing on your site.

Mobile publishing

Thus far this chapter has concentrated mostly on digital production for the web, but for a number of brands the more important leap is less the web itself than the ability to view content stylishly on a mobile device. At its simplest, this may be little more than a web page being reformatted correctly for a tablet or phone, but more sophisticated titles will also seek to create apps that can display a magazine natively, rather than through the browser.

In 2014, the digital analytics company comScore (comscore.com) released a white paper showing that 88 per cent of activity on smartphones was via apps rather than through a browser – although in the same year the Interactive Advertising Bureau (IAB, iab.com) produced an apparently contradictory report that, following a survey of users, found only 18 per cent of them strongly favoured apps. Some further digging reveals that these two reports may not be such polar opposites as they first appear; in the IAB survey, one of the main factors affecting users' preference was the cost of apps, meaning that often they would use the mobile web in preference over a paid alternative – but it is still extremely likely that once they have downloaded a particular set of apps, such as for social media or a game, then most of their activity is via them rather than through the browser.

At the time of writing, certain functions, such as finding news, show no clear distinction between the mobile web and apps, but with the rise and rise of mobile and ever sleeker apps appearing on tablets and phones it is likely that apps will become ever more important. As such, designing for apps – either taking advantage of a third-party provider or building one from scratch – is becoming ever more essential.

Of the various routes towards mobile publishing, the simplest – and least recommended – is simply to port a PDF of the title to be downloaded through an app such as Zinio (zinio.com). In essence, this simply cuts out the process of printing the title and production more or less follows the pattern outlined in the previous chapter, with some minor considerations such as less reliance on colour separation. The reason that this is not recommended is that the surface area of even the largest tablets (and certainly all phones) is hugely different to that of a typical printed magazine, so that a beautifully designed print page can appear cramped and ugly on a mobile device.

Of the other alternatives, creating an app from scratch is a complex activity requiring some knowledge of coding that is far beyond the remit of this particular book. Instead, the rest of this chapter will consider the means of publishing a title using third-party software.

Platforms

The first consideration when designing an app is which platform to publish on, with the three main contenders currently being Apple's iOS, Google's Android and, perhaps, Microsoft's Windows 10 (previously Windows Phone). By early 2015, the market analysts International Data Corporation (idc.com) observed that Android dominated the smartphone market with an 82.8 per cent share, followed by Apple's iOS at 13.9 per cent. Microsoft, which had absorbed Nokia's mobile business into its main activities, barely scraped above 2 per cent. Indeed, as so many software companies do not even bother to release apps for Windows, many commentators have announced that the platform is effectively dead.

As such, the main competition would appear to be between iOS and Android and, with such a huge lead, one would expect publishers to focus their efforts on Google's platform. The logic of the raw numbers outlined above would suggest that anyone wishing to reach the most brands should concentrate on the devices that most readers use.

Yet in fact, many developers concentrate on Apple's mobile devices first. iOS may not be the most popular platform, but Apple's phones are the second-most popular in the world after Samsung's – and by far the most profitable. Indeed, when considering the share of profits as opposed to that of unit sales, by the end of 2015 Apple was capturing a record 94 per cent of smartphone profits according to data from Canaccord Genuity. The iPhone is an aspirational device, and as other manufacturers cut their prices to try and remain competitive Apple appears to rise above the melee, for all that it may have reached peak distribution.

As iPhones are more expensive, so their users tend to have more cash to spend on things such as apps. One of the reasons developers prefer iOS to Android is that, as is shown again and again in various surveys, they make more money from software produced for Apple. App Annie (appannie.com) analysed data from the iOS App Store and Google Play and found that while nearly twice as many apps were downloaded from the latter in 2015, the ratio for the amount of revenue generated from those apps was reversed.

Income generated from sales, however, is only one part of the cost to developers. When designing for mobile, a focus on iOS means that brands only have to focus on a limited range of formats and screen resolutions. Android, however, is an immensely fragmented market, with phones ranging from less than $100 to just under $800 (ignoring, for a moment, lavish titanium, gold and even diamond-encrusted models); these in turn have screens that can span resolutions anywhere between 320 × 240 pixels to 2560 × 1440 (known as Quad HD). A properly designed app has to look good on all of these, and inevitably developers will leave out many of the smallest resolutions.

To make matters worse, there is no guarantee as to what software will actually be running on an Android device. By the beginning of 2016, Apple's latest version of iOS, 9, was running on 75 per cent of active devices. Against this, very few devices had received Google's latest update to Android, version 6 (or 'Marshmallow'); instead 23.5 per cent were running version 5 ('Lollipop'), 38.9 version 4 ('Kitkat') and an incredible 37.6 a version that was more than two years old. A developer creating software for the many millions of Android devices in the world can quickly run into headaches when trying to take advantage of the most recent improvements to Google's operating system.

This outline of the choices facing developers is not a simple promotion of iOS over Android. Certainly iOS is easier to develop for than Android, but to focus on that entirely at the expense of phones built on Google's platform means that while a brand can reach the most affluent readers, it is also likely to miss four out of five members of its possible audience. This is why the mobile web remains so important to magazines in the end: developing apps for Android can be an expensive and time-consuming business, but it is still extremely important to get content out to readers.

Publishing tools

When designing for mobile, there are a number of options available to publishers that do not require them to build an app from scratch. Some of these are designed to fit into the workflow that has built up around DTP software for print, and some make use of developments in HTML5 to produce mobile-friendly web apps. In addition, there is also the possibility that publishers can take advantage of discrete apps or marketplaces such as Zinio or Flipboard which bring together content in a variety of ways.

Figure 6.5 Zinio is a popular cross-platform app for delivering digital magazines

For a traditional publishing house, one of the most obvious solutions is Adobe's Digital Publishing Suite (DPS). This is an immensely sophisticated package that integrates fully with Adobe's other products such as InDesign and Photoshop, allowing magazines to draw upon a wealth of talent that they can use to make sophisticated apps that will be fully interactive on a mobile device and can be published to the App Store, Google Play and even Amazon. It is the software used to produce titles such as *National Geographic* and *Top Gear*, and is much more than an export option to churn out PDFs. Options are arranged as an extra panel within InDesign, so it fully integrates with a typical workflow, allowing artists to create animations and touch-activated transitions that can be a joy to navigate and fully tested before they are published online.

As so many magazines use production staff who are familiar with Adobe products, this would surely seem to be the obvious path to follow to create a media-rich magazine. The main obstacle is price: to create a magazine with multiple editions requires an annual subscription to the Professional Edition, currently listed at more than €5,000. QuarkXPress, which has lost a great deal of ground to Adobe in recent years, offers an alternative App Studio plug-in, although its professional edition for multiple editions still nudges the €5,000 price tag.

Because publishers have struggled to make digital editions profitable, this has meant a burgeoning business in alternatives to Adobe and Quark. Some of these, such as Mag+ (magplus.com) are very similar to Adobe DPS, working as

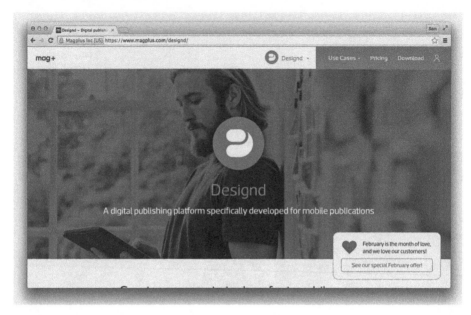

Figure 6.6 Mag+ is one of a new generation of tools for publishing to mobile

a plug-in for InDesign that can capitalise on typical magazine workflows; as with DPS, it is free to download and use, with costs being charged when the finished title is uploaded as an app. Publishing via Mag+ is not hugely cheaper than DPS if regular updates are required (costing $499 per month at the time of writing), although there is the option to publish a one-off title for $999. Mag+ is extremely good software, with some of its tools allowing drag-and-drop design for interactive titles, and it has been widely used by brands such as *Forbes* and *New York Magazine*, but its pricing has not made it especially popular in comparison with DPS for commercial publishers. Some of the same caveats apply to Aquafadas (aquafadas.com/en/), another InDesign plug-in that has an annual subscription price of over $4,000 but with cheaper options for educational use restricted to 1,000 readers.

In addition to software that allows publishers to create a separate app, there are also some services that will create a magazine as part of a host app or market-place. These include MagCloud (magcloud.com) and Joomag (joomag.com). Both of these allow publishers to create platform-neutral, fully interactive titles, handling distribution through their own apps for Android and iOS. The downside of this for mainstream commercial publishers is that there is little control over the ultimate branding of a title, and none of the big com-petitors publishes this way, but it can be an extremely cost-effective way for independent publishers to test out digital editions of their titles. MagCloud, for example, allows magazines to be distributed entirely for free and then takes 50 per cent of the price when the magazine charges for content. Joomag similarly allows users to upload a PDF or create a fully interactive version through the web site; the free version, hosted via Joomag's own app, will carry ads for the company, but subscriptions to remove those ads start from $15.95 per month. Although the final product is not as slick as something created via DPS or Mag+, essentially being an HTML5 page that is hosted on the company's servers and so is not as smooth-running as a native app, it offers a very good means to begin exploring the world of digital publishing for mobile.

7
Legal and ethical issues

Many of the regulatory issues that affect magazines are similar to those across the media industry. This chapter offers a summary of the legal restraints that all editors and publishers have to consider with regard to defamation, copyright, data protection, fair comment and privacy. For a more detailed consideration of legal issues, the reader should also consult *McNae's Essential Law for Journalists* (Dodd and Hanna 2015).

Some areas of legislation, such as Defence Advisory (DA) Notices, the Human Rights Act and court reporting, are generally more important to newspapers than magazines (other than specialist interest titles), and so are not dealt with in any great detail here. As well as the law, however, journalists also need to consider ethical and professional codes of conduct for the material that they publish.

Defamation

Laws against defamation, principally the UK Defamation Act 2013, are intended to protect the reputation of an individual against unjustified and unwarranted attacks. Any communication that is held to damage a reputation is considered defamatory even if it is fiction, meaning that such things as television plays and magazine short stories fall under the remit of the law if they are seen to harm an individual.

While there have been various criticisms of the harshness of the UK defamatory laws, in principle their purpose is to balance the right of a person to protect his or her reputation against the defence of freedom of speech and expression. As Mason and Smith observe (1998: 8; original emphasis):

> The real skill in journalism does not show simply in the cleverness of the ways of defending an action for defamation ... but in recognising a possible problem *before publication*, and then in handling it in such a

way that any complaint after publication can be successfully rebutted or defended.

The maxim should be: 'If in doubt find out' rather than 'If in doubt leave it out'.

Defamation is held to have taken place if a person is exposed to hatred, contempt or ridicule, is shunned or avoided after publication, discredited in a business or profession, and generally lowered in the eyes of the public in an unwarranted fashion.

Unlike other criminal and civil actions, where burden of proof rests on the prosecution or plaintiff, in UK libel laws the burden of proof rests on the defendant. The plaintiff does have to prove, however, that any defamatory statements will be reasonably understood to refer to him or her, and that they are communicated to a third person (which is not difficult in the case of libel as words are recorded in print or other permanent form).

The previous 1996 Defamation Act cleared up one important area regarding who could be sued: in the past, this could be anyone involved in distribution of material, such as printers and newsagents, but since 1996 this has been restricted to the authors, editors or publishers of defamatory material.

What is more, the author of a defamatory statement is the person who originated that statement, but may defend him- or herself if that statement was never intended for publication, for example in a private diary.

Libel and slander

There are two types of defamation: slander, which is a communication by word of mouth, and libel, which relates to publication in print or a more permanent form such as a broadcast.

Libel is more serious for a magazine because obviously that deals with publication. In addition, slander needs to be made in the presence of witnesses for a prosecution to succeed. A journalist may still slander an individual, however, for example, simply by talking about someone in the presence of others in a defamatory manner or via telephone calls to a third party.

In libel cases the plaintiff does not need to prove that he or she suffered monetary losses as a result of the publication, although slander does require this proof unless they have been accused of a criminal action, or attacked on the basis of their profession. In both libel and slander, the plaintiff may bring a case even if they have not been named. If it is held that a reasonable individual could infer the identity of the person from an article or statement, then the law is likely to uphold their complaint.

Truth and privilege

The ultimate defence against libel is truth, referred to legally as justification: a statement may be damaging to an individual's reputation, but if it is true then it is not defamatory. However, if the statement refers to a conviction regarded as 'spent' under the Rehabilitation of Offenders Act 1974, or is a criminal libel, it may be considered libellous if prompted through malice.

Criminal libel is rarely invoked in the UK, unless the libel is held to be so serious that criminal proceedings will best serve the public interest. Mason and Smith give the example of allegations in *Private Eye* in 1975 that were seen to link Sir James Goldsmith to Lord Lucan, then the subject of a murder investigation. The case was dropped when *Private Eye* withdrew the statements and publicly apologised.

Libel proceedings cannot be brought against the dead in civil law (which covers most cases in the UK), although it is possible under criminal libel if statements are shown to affect living relatives or potentially cause a breach of the peace.

Journalists may publish defamatory material safely under the defence of absolute or qualified privilege. The first relates to reporting court cases that deal with alleged crimes, where journalists must be protected from the threat of defamation in order to report what they see as the truth. However, if a journalist reports evidence ruled as inadmissible, he or she may be guilty of contempt of court, and so in danger of prosecution.

Qualified privilege covers reports of public proceedings, such as public inquiries and conferences, as well as court cases, as well as documents required to be open to public inspection such as statements produced by members of government. However, the defence of qualified privilege might be lost if reporting is shown to be motivated by malice or is inaccurate. Likewise, if the plaintiff asked for a contradictory statement to be published (denying any defamatory comments) and this is not included in publication, qualified privilege may also be revoked.

Malicious falsehoods and fair comment

While issues of absolute and qualified privilege tend to affect newspaper journalists more than those working for magazines, this is not the case for reviewers, who may often be affected by cases brought against them.

When testing or reviewing products, journalists, editors and publishers may face a prosecution for malicious falsehood, sometimes called 'trade libels'. If a review disparages the goods that a person produces or trades in a defamatory manner, it is not a libel but a malicious falsehood. If, however, the review goes on to suggest incorrectly that the fault of the goods is due to the professional character of that person, then it becomes a libel.

In a case of malicious falsehood, the burden of proof that a statement is untrue falls on the plaintiff, who must also demonstrate damages such as financial loss. In addition, malice must be proved in this type of case, and while a libel suit ends with the death of either the plaintiff or defendant, cases of malicious falsehood can be carried on by representatives of the deceased.

Defence against malicious falsehood requires the defendant to prove the accuracy of any tests he or she may have carried out, following any instructions regarding testing to the letter. When making adverse claims against competing products, the reviewer should be certain that he or she is really comparing like with like.

While malicious falsehood tends to refer to product testing, libel is more likely to be invoked for other types of reviews where an individual is involved, for example music or film reviewing.

In such cases, a reviewer may be able to invoke the defence of fair comment: this means that the reviewer offered his or her honest opinion of events, persons or products (including the fact that he or she did not like them, or believe them of suitable quality – the most important task of the reviewer as we saw in Chapter 4). However, this cannot be used as a defence if the journalist gets facts wrong or if comments can be shown to be irresponsible or motivated by malice.

Professional indemnity

This chapter has considered libel and malicious falsehood in some detail because the consequences of getting it wrong can be very serious for a publication. Payments can be severely damaging to the reputation of a title as well as its finances. Roman Polanski won £50,000 in a libel suit from *Vanity Fair* for an article in 2002 that made him appear 'callously indifferent', in his words, to the death of his former wife, Sharon Tate. More recently *Star* magazine paid undisclosed damages in an out-of-court settlement to the actor Katie Holmes after running a headline that implied drug misuse.

Sometimes libel payments can run to extremes. An Indonesian court ordered *Time* magazine to pay more than $100 million in damages for an article about former President Suharto, although *Time* was still contesting that action. It is more common for libel payments to be revised downwards, for example from £600,000 to £60,000 paid by *Private Eye* to Sonia Sutcliffe, wife of the Yorkshire Ripper.

Yet damages are only part of the problem for titles faced with a libel suit. In another case, again with *Private Eye* (one of the most sued magazines in the world), a suit brought by a Cornish accountant against the magazine was thrown out of court because the plaintiff, Stuart Condliffe, declared himself bankrupt and was thus unable to pay legal fees.

Because of this, there are several legal companies that offer Professional Indemnity and Public Liability Insurance. In most cases, this will offer to cover potential costs in the case of libel, but also protection for infringement of copyright and breach of confidentiality.

While this offers a degree of reassurance to a number of publishers and editors (and increasingly writers who find that they may be sued), some working in the industry consider insurance to be a double-edged sword. Because of the threat of high legal costs, insurers will often wish to settle before the matter comes to court – which for a combative editor who may wish to see the case through can become extremely problematic.

Copyright

Copyright is essential to publishing – without it, publishers would not be able to make a profit from the materials they produce. Copyright law in the UK dates back to the Statute of Anne 1709, but became statutory law in 1911 with the passing of the Copyright Act, itself modified in the Copyright, Designs, Patent Act 1988. This was further modified by the Copyright and Related Rights Regulations 2003, which dealt with copying electronic documents.

Beyond the UK, there is no single standard law that operates the same way in every country, but there are several international treaties that have their basis in the 1886 Berne Convention.

Copyright, as the UK Intellectual Property Office points out, is a private right that enables the creator of a work, whether produced as a written text, music, film or broadcast, to decide how it is distributed. It is in place to protect the outcome of a person's labour and, as intellectual property, can be bought and sold or transferred to a third party. This is what often happens when a publisher (whether of literature, music or film) buys the rights to a particular work.

Intellectual property rights exist independently of the work they protect and are assigned automatically. There is no official registration system in the UK (or most of the rest of the world), although publishers in various media will often mark a work as under copyright with the symbol ©. This allows readers and other users to know that a work has entered the period of copyright, and so illegal copies cannot be made and distributed.

Terms of copyright

To come under the terms of copyright, a work must be original. This is not the same as saying that the work has never been done before, but that it exists in a unique form. Facts or ideas themselves cannot be copyrighted, but the particular expression of these can attract copyright protection. In the UK, a single word is not sufficient to compose a work covered by copyright, although a phrase may be registered as a trade mark.

Since August 1989, after the 1988 Act came into place, copyright belongs with the author in the first instance – and not the person who commissioned the work as often was the case previously. However, for work produced as part of employment, such as by a staff writer, copyright now belongs to the employer. Freelances may be employed for a specific piece of work (a contract *for* service), which means that they own copyright unless this is specifically negotiated by the editor. Alternatively, if they work for a publisher for a period of time (a contract *of* service) then copyright for all their work done under that contract belongs to the employer, even if it is done at home.

For literary, dramatic, musical or artistic works, as well as films, the duration of the copyright is 70 years after the author's death or, if the author is unknown, 70 years after the period when it was made available to the public. Duration of copyright for sound recordings and broadcasts is 50 years from the year in which the work was made, and typographical arrangements have a duration of 25 years from the date they were created.

Moral rights

Under the 1988 Act, an author is ascribed moral rights to a work, although this affects journalists much less than other producers, whether literary or in other media, because of certain exceptions.

Moral rights mean that the author has the right to be identified as such – a work cannot be published under another name if the author does not agree. In addition, a work cannot be modified without the author's permission, and certainly not in a derogatory way that will diminish his or her reputation.

However, because of the difficulties of producing work for magazines and newspapers to tight deadlines and with many writers, exceptions were written into the Act. Moral rights, therefore, do not apply to an employee's work, or for those made for publication in periodicals or collected reference works. Without this, anyone producing even a short news paragraph would have to receive a byline, and subs would not be able to make changes without the author's express permission.

Fair dealing

Under copyright laws, it is an offence to copy a work, rent, lend or perform it in any way to the public, or adapt it.

However, there are conditions under which it is possible to make limited use of a work that will not infringe its rights, what is known as 'fair dealing'. Thus a work can be used for private and research study purposes, and lending for educational purposes. It is also possible to copy parts of a work when engaged in criticism and news reporting, and incidental reproductions (for example, a poster in the background of a photograph) are protected.

There are also certain other users, not relevant to print magazines, where fair dealing comes into play, such as the ability of non-profit making organisations to play sound recordings. Also, changes from 2003 made it illegal to produce copies of documents for commercial purposes (exceptions that had previously been allowed).

In practice, journalists will not be sued for copyright infringement when using quotes so long as these do not constitute a major part of their article. Conventionally, fair dealing has been taken to mean up to 400 words in one extract, or 800 words in a series of extracts (none of which should be more than 250 words individually).

Intellectual property rights and digital media

Although not the subject of a book on print magazines in themselves, the most recent controversies around copyright relate to distribution and dissemination of material on the internet. While the biggest problems relating to infringement of copyright have affected music publishers and film studios, with the move by a number of publishers onto the World Wide Web this does remain an area of concern.

At root, the difficulty of new technologies for publishers of traditional media is twofold. First, older means of copying (such as audio tape or photocopying) nearly always incurred an inevitable degradation between the original and the copy. With digital media, it is possible to create a perfect, or near-perfect, copy almost instantly.

Second, the distribution of different products such as video cassettes, books and printed magazines meant that the effort of manufacturing and selling copyrighted work on a large scale was difficult. This is not the same as impossible, and indeed a big market for pirated materials remains in the distribution of illegal DVDs, for example. However, the ease with which electronic data can be passed between international borders has created difficulties for producers who wish to enforce intellectual property rights around the world, particularly in emerging markets such as China or parts of Eastern Europe.

The most strenuous responses against what has been seen as a threat from new media have been the US Digital Millennium Copyright Act (DMCA) 1998 and the EU Copyright Directive (EUCD) 2001 (implemented in the UK as the Copyright and Related Rights Regulations 2003). Each of these similar Acts placed severe restrictions upon any attempt to circumvent copyright restrictions through the use of new technologies. More recently, however, attempts have been made to reform these bills which are often seen by opponents as anti-competitive, having reduced the right of the consumer to fair use.

Confidential information

There may be times when a journalist comes into possession of confidential information which must be handled sensitively. The basis of laws surrounding confidentiality in the UK is largely a result of judgments in common law rather than statutes passed by Parliament, although the Human Rights Act 1998, which came into effect in 2000, did give qualified rights to protect information from private life, but not if there is a threat in terms of crime or public health.

To be confidential, information must not be in the public domain in any way – so while a company may protect its trade secrets, if these have been registered for a patent then disseminating that information does not break any laws of confidentiality. Traditionally, the law of confidentiality protects personal information, government secrets and trade secrets. Usually it is information that is commercial in some degree, but can also cover material that relates to personal morality or is of a sexual nature.

Outside of information unlawfully obtained, confidentiality can affect journalists in other ways. First of all, there is a question of confidential sources: sometimes a reporter will have information the source of which he or she does not want to reveal in any way. Before the Contempt of Court Act 1981, journalists could go to prison for failing to reveal those sources when ordered by a judge, but since then a court can only require disclosure if national security is threatened, or if disclosure is necessary in the interests of preventing disorder or crime.

This type of situation is very rare for magazine (as opposed to newspaper) journalists. More commonly, they may encounter information that is given to them 'off the record'. If a source does not wish to be identified, the writer should exercise caution: if journalists include non-attributable material, the motivation of the source needs to be questioned. It should also be thoroughly checked – particularly if there is a danger of publishing potentially libellous statements.

Finally, journalists may frequently be asked to sign a non-disclosure agreement (NDA), particularly if they work for a B2B magazine. This is a legal contract between a magazine and other source, usually a PR agency or company, requiring the title not to disclose certain information shared for a particular purpose.

Typically, a company will have a new product or service that they wish to reveal to the public at a particular time. Under such circumstances they may approach several publications and provide advance information that is not to be published before a certain date. Often they will contain a penalty clause, outlining the compensation that will be paid if there is a breach of confidence.

Data protection and freedom of information

With the passing of the Data Protection Act 1998, certain types of information have been given statutory protection in the UK. It relates to personal information, rather than trade or government secrets, and applies across all types of businesses, not just magazines.

Under the Act, individuals have a wide range of rights, including access to any information held about them, the right to correct that information, protection from unsolicited marketing and the ability to claim compensation. It does not protect individual privacy at all costs, but does try to balance those needs against the often legitimate requirements of a company or organisation to hold information.

For magazines, data protection often affects other departments more than editorial, in that as a company a publication will collect considerable amounts of data of a personal nature on subscribers and readers. As such, a magazine must be sure that anyone it collects information from is aware of why and how that data is held, and ensure that it is correct and up to date.

Once such information is no longer reasonably usable (for example, in the case of subscribers who have cancelled and no longer wish to purchase a title), it should be destroyed. There are also strict limits placed on what can be done with this information in terms of selling it to third parties. The Act is regulated by the Information Commissioner's Office.

Another law affecting the use of information is the Freedom of Information (FOI) Act 2000, which gives people access to information held by public bodies (a separate Act was passed for Scotland in 2002). Previously, government information was often closed off to the public for a standard 30-year period, but now it is considered open from the start unless exemptions apply. These exemptions include issues of national security, law enforcement and investigations by public authorities among other things.

Those wishing to discover information held in the National Archive or in departmental bodies do so by sending a written request (letter, fax or email) to the FOI authority. If they are not happy with the response, they can complain to the Information Commissioner's Office as the independent regulator of the Act.

Privacy

In contrast to relatively clear laws governing the communication of data, there is no law that protects an individual's privacy as it would commonly be understood when intruded upon by the media. Despite some high-profile cases in recent years, such as those of Catherine Zeta Jones and Michael Douglas against *Hello!* in 2003 (the outcome of which was actually overturned by the House of Lords in 2005, then reinstated in 2007) and an award to the Radio 1 presenter Sara Cox (actually settled out of court after the *People* published pictures of her and her husband nude while on honeymoon in the Seychelles) that may, in the words of one judge, be creating a privacy law 'bit by bit', there is still no overarching law protecting personal privacy.

In December 2007, Sienna Miller received what was believed to be the largest payment of its kind for an invasion of privacy – £37,500 in damages – after the *News of the World* published nude pictures of her. More importantly in terms of the development of privacy laws, however, has been the emergence of so-called 'super-injunctions', a term coined by the *Guardian* in 2009 to describe events surrounding reporting of the Trafigura controversy. Trafigura, a Dutch multinational commodity trading company, had been involved in a number of scandals but an injunction applied for by the London libel lawyers Carter Ruck prevented the newspaper from reporting not simply on the scandals themselves, but also that an injunction had been applied in this particular case. The suspicion that this aroused among the general public eventually led a spokesperson for the government to emphasise that the Parliamentary Papers Act of 1840, which gives absolute privilege against criminal and civil proceedings to publications made under the House of Commons' authority and qualified privilege to publications circulating extracts of parliamentary papers, remained in place.

Interest in extending laws on privacy in the UK first began to gain ground in March 1993, when a Commons national heritage committee on privacy and media intrusion included in its 43 recommendations that the government appoint a press ombudsman and introduce a Protection of Privacy Bill. Furthermore, in 1995, a House of Commons Select Committee had recommended that should such a law exist, it would protect personal information and also preserve a person from harassment. The first part has, to a lesser or greater extent, been covered by data protection laws, but the latter is still largely governed by self-regulation rather than legislation. The Human Rights Act, however, does give protection to some areas of private and family life.

The most recent version of the IPSO Code of Practice, ratified in March 2015, states under clause 3 on 'Privacy' that 'Editors will be expected to justify intrusions into any individual's private life without consent'. In addition, it states that photographs should not be taken of individuals in private places without their consent, and (in clause 4 under the heading 'Harassment') that 'Journalists must not engage in intimidation, harassment or persistent pursuit'.

However, there are a number of clauses in the code to which there may be exceptions where the breach of the code can be demonstrated to be in the public interest, and so complaints to IPSO are not always upheld.

Stories held to be in the public interest include: those in which a crime or serious impropriety may be exposed; where public health and safety needs to be protected; and where the public needs to be protected from being misled by an individual or organisation. In addition, there is a very wide-ranging exception in that the code states: 'There is a public interest in freedom of expression itself.'

Where there is an appeal to public interest, IPSO expects a publication to demonstrate how that interest was fulfilled. In such cases, journalists have to take into account when a private person becomes a public figure. Celebrities, politicians and members of the royal family are clearly open to public scrutiny, although even in those cases IPSO may uphold complaints when a publication has failed to take into account their right to a private life.

The IPSO Code of Practice has barely changed since its previous incarnation as part of the Press Complaints Commission (PCC). While in part this demonstrates that its recommendations follow common sense in many regards, it is more problematic considering the nature of IPSO's formation. Set up in September 2014 to replace the PCC, IPSO was one response to the extensive inquiry by Lord Justice Leveson into abuses by the British press following the *News of the World* phone-hacking scandal. One outcome of that inquiry was a condemnation of the PCC as insufficient and a Royal Charter on self-regulation of the press was issued which the news industry largely ignored, pushing for IPSO instead. Unlike the PCC, IPSO does have the power to fine publishers for systematic wrongdoing, but groups such as Hacked Off (which pushed for the Leveson Inquiry) have been critical of its work.

Copy approval

Piers Morgan in his diaries, *The Insider*, commented that copy approval, the practice of allowing a third party, such as an interviewee or company, the right to see information about them before it goes to print, 'is a hidden shame . . . that has grown in recent years to be an epidemic' (2005: 308).

The difficulty for a large number of publications, particularly tabloid newspapers and celebrity magazines, is that they need interviews with famous (or even not-so-famous) people to sell their issues, but those figures are unlikely to agree unless they can see and approve copy beforehand. Even B2B titles can find themselves in the position of having to negotiate deals with companies and organisations, and PR agencies will always wish to view copy before it is published.

It is perfectly reasonable for someone working in PR to want to view information about their client, to capitalise on good news or prepare for the worst. However, it is more than equally reasonable for an editor to refuse.

The most sensible position – if not always the easiest – is to issue a blanket refusal on all copy approval. This might result in missed 'scoops', but it will make the editorial department's job much easier in the long run: once it becomes known that a title agreed to show material prior to publication to one individual or organisation, then plenty of others will want the same privilege. Of course, when issuing such a blanket refusal there is greater responsibility on the journalist to be accurate and fair.

Codes of conduct

As well as the threat of legal action, the practice of journalism is also subject to professional codes of conduct, ways of acting that are considered best practice. Many individual publications will issue their own codes to staff, ways of behaving at work that they feel are essential to the job, and many countries around the world (especially in Europe and North America) have long-established national codes that are adopted by journalists working in the profession.

In the UK, the NUJ provides a code of professional behaviour that may be viewed at www.nuj.org.uk. The most recent version, updated in 2011, runs as follows:

A journalist

1   At all times upholds and defends the principle of media freedom, the right of freedom of expression and the right of the public to be informed.
2   Strives to ensure that information disseminated is honestly conveyed, accurate and fair.
3   Does her/his utmost to correct harmful inaccuracies.
4   Differentiates between fact and opinion.
5   Obtains material by honest, straightforward and open means, with the exception of investigations that are both overwhelmingly in the public interest and which involve evidence that cannot be obtained by straightforward means.
6   Does nothing to intrude into anybody's private life, grief or distress unless justified by overriding consideration of the public interest.
7   Protects the identity of sources who supply information in confidence and material gathered in the course of her/his work.
8   Resists threats or any other inducements to influence, distort or suppress information and takes no unfair personal advantage of information gained in the course of her/his duties before the information is public knowledge.
9   Produces no material likely to lead to hatred or discrimination on the grounds of a person's age, gender, race, colour, creed, legal status, disability, marital status, or sexual orientation.
10 Does not by way of statement, voice or appearance endorse by advertisement any commercial product or service save for the promotion of her/his own work or of the medium by which she/he is employed.
11 A journalist shall normally seek the consent of an appropriate adult when interviewing or photographing a child for a story about her/his welfare.
12 Avoids plagiarism.

The NUJ code also provides an important final note:

The NUJ believes the journalist has a right to refuse an assignment or to be identified as the author of editorial that would break the letter or spirit of the code. The NUJ will fully support any journalist disciplined for asserting his/her right to act according to the code.

This notion of a 'conscience clause' featured prominently in the NUJ's submission to Leveson and was supported by Leveson in his final report.

In addition to the NUJ code, IPSO issues its own code with which every journalist should be familiar, and which can be viewed at www.ipso.co.uk/ IPSO/cop.html. This covers ethical standards to which publications and journalists should adhere if they wish to avoid censure in the areas of accuracy, the right to reply, privacy and harassment, reporting on children, reporting crime, the use of clandestine devices to obtain information, financial journalism and payment to criminals or witnesses in criminal trials.

Complaints and the right to reply

Sometimes a magazine can get things wrong, and sometimes a reader might feel that a magazine has got things wrong. The two are not always the same, but an editor should have a policy in place to deal with both types of complaint.

Even if a mistake has happened, this does not automatically mean that legal action can, or should, be taken. In any case, in the first instance when a complaint is received, the initial course of action should not be automatically to apologise, as this could be taken as an admission of liability. The first step, if the complainant is making contact via phone, is to take notes but also to ask them to confirm the complaint in writing. After this, the editor should go about collecting relevant information about the article in question, such as any interviews, emails or other documents.

Once a complaint has been received in writing, then it must be addressed more formally. Again, the automatic route should not be simply to issue an apology either by letter or in print, but to determine what the facts of the case are. If a claim is without substance, then the editor has to stand firm; to do otherwise could itself prompt further demands and even claims of libel.

If the magazine is in error, then the next step may be to publish a correction or apology. Attempts to be reasonable can be helpful in a court case, but of themselves they do not remove the need for a suit if, for example, the complainant believes that he or she has been libelled.

When publishing a correction or apology, this does need to be seen and agreed by the complainant. A condition of publication should be that the complainant will also provide a written statement accepting the apology as full and final settlement. If an editor or in publisher has to engage in communication with the complainant in cases that are likely to become aggravated, then letters are best sent through a lawyer and marked clearly 'without prejudice', so that they cannot be used as evidence in a legal action.

While the gravest concern of an editor must be lawsuits that could be very costly, there will be plenty of other times when a magazine is approached with complaints that have less serious consequences but need to be handled sensitively. Plenty of readers will want to complain to the editor when they do not receive their subscription, for example, but such details have to be passed on to the appropriate department. Likewise, the prevalence of readers' pages is a good opportunity to demonstrate a magazine's ability to respond to the needs of its readers, as a sounding board for things they do not like as well as those they do.

8
Conclusion

The future of magazines

Since the first edition of this book, magazines have undergone a long – and often difficult – decade of change. In 2007, while an increasing number of brands had web sites, these were almost entirely peripheral to the core business of publishing which was resolutely print in most areas. There were a few exceptions, most notably in the technology sector which, unsurprisingly, had to move online more quickly as its readers sought out information through the web. Similarly, social media was still in its early stages and Apple had only just launched the iPhone, the device that would do most to revolutionise mobile platforms.

Now, at the beginning of 2016, an increasing number of titles are considering digital-only publications and mobile is especially important to them and their readers. This is not to underestimate the power of print: unlike newspapers, which more rapidly lost consumers for their print editions, glossy magazines for a long time still seemed the favourite format for a majority of readers and that still remains the case today. Yet the drastic decline of some niche markets has already resulted in a thinning out of the magazine sector and has forced sometimes reluctant publishers to consider the alternatives. According to the PPA's *Publishing Futures* survey of 2015, while print remains a core activity for brands the most important priority is optimising content for mobile.

Even just five years ago, the outlook for many in the industry could have looked grim, but as we have seen with several examples in this book, such as *The Economist* and *National Geographic*, the move to digital has opened up huge possibilities that have led several publishers to be extremely optimistic about the next decade. Groups such as Condé Nast and Hearst Magazines are making considerable investments into the magazine sector, but the big growth from now on will be in digital. Print is far from dead – *Vogue*'s 98th year as a magazine was also its most profitable – but now brands are looking to expand in areas such as ecommerce and elearning as well as digital publishing.

Branding success

The main factor behind those titles that have weathered the recent difficulties has been quality. One of the reasons (in the UK at least) for a relative collapse of magazine circulations was the decline of celebrity titles such as *Heat* and *Hello!*. With the rise of sites such as Twitter, and the possibility of gaining some access into the lives of celebrities more directly, weekly publications began to look very stale. For anyone seeking celebrity gossip, a site such as *TMZ* (tmz.com) has instant appeal and it is always going to be easier to find news via a mobile app than inside the pages of a magazine.

Similarly, many of those brands that were aimed at a younger audience have seen readers drift away to blogs and video-sharing sites like YouTube. Figures such as Felix Kjellberg, better known as PewDiePie, or Michelle Phan have millions of subscribers and attract hundreds of thousands of views for each video they post and in some cases have become millionaires through their activities. As well as displaying a degree of entrepreneurial nous (Phan has released her own cosmetics range, for example), they are young and speak to their audiences in an easy-going, natural style that has immense appeal for a generation of digital natives.

The late twentieth century saw a fragmentation of media that has only become more diverse in the twenty-first. And yet for magazines this is also a moment of opportunity. After a shaky period between 2010 and 2012, many companies are reporting increasing profits and have begun to promote themselves much more actively online and through more traditional channels. Visibility is key, and while there are some stars who make it to the top through social media behind these are vast numbers of hopefuls who struggle to connect with an audience.

This is why quality is so important. On a personal level, the current shakeout of the magazine market is not entirely surprising, nor even unwelcome, to me. Throughout the nineties it seemed that too many titles were in a race to the bottom to attract readers, and for any reader hoping to catch a glimpse of a celebrity's cellulite there are plenty of opportunities online that need not bother us here. Elsewhere, magazine staples such as fashion and beauty or newer markets such as video gaming are extremely well served by a new generation of media stars who grasp intuitively what younger audiences desire and need.

In many areas, however, the best-performing magazines demonstrate that there is still a hunger for good-quality journalism. In less glamorous markets such as the B2B sector, readers still have to know what is happening in the world, and there are plenty of areas where getting that information requires more than an individual sitting in front of a camera. Rather than focusing on external threats, the PPA 2015 survey found that an increasing number of publishers were now turning to internal challenges – changing their company structures, improving their IT, hiring new staff with relevant skills – that would help them look outwards to the changing market. In many cases, this is not simply to do new things but to do old things better, to concentrate on what works.

Curating content

As brands, magazines that embrace the shift to digital have a head start in finding visibility in the digital world. Yet the future could mean that some of the fundamental attitudes that have shaped magazines over the past century will have to change. At the moment, many publishers have sought to move into digital editions, and indeed mobile platforms are the major way in which consumers engage with all sorts of media.

Yet this is not a simple shift from one format (print) to another (mobile). Too many publishers have relied on the traditional workflows they built up for monthly or weekly titles that have served them well to now, with the result that they have tended simply to ship out PDFs of their printed pages, a format that has largely been unsuccessful. Some of those that have invested heavily in app development have seen some return on their investments. Leaving aside *The Economist* (which still combines print and digital for many of its readers), titles such as *Top Gear*, *Empire* and *GQ* have managed to achieve circulations above 10,000 for their digital editions, but by the end of 2015 for many titles the spurt of growth after investment began in 2011 is starting to turn into decline.

Part of the problem has been a failure to take digital as seriously as print, but there have also been other factors, such as the collapse of Apple's Newsstand, which shows that publishers need to make further changes. The situation is perhaps best illustrated by the example of the music industry. For most of the twentieth century it relied on albums to drive sales and profits, a clear, easy-to-understand format that appeared to offer value to listeners in comparison with singles (which could be seen as advertisements for the main product), and that had a highly structured form in terms of distribution. Vinyl and then CD made sense, and a 72-minute album was designed for those formats.

With the move to online consumption, however, first through illegal peer-to-peer sharing and then through channels such as iTunes or streaming sites, listeners have shown again and again that the single track is often their preferred format. Many people would often buy an album simply because they wanted to listen to one or two tracks that were not easily available elsewhere; once these could be downloaded for 99 cents or as part of a monthly subscription, so album sales inevitably declined. Something similar is happening with television content through sites and apps such as Netflix or Amazon Prime.

It is clear that there are plenty of readers who desire high-quality articles. In a few cases, they may even be willing to pay for them directly, though for the large part advertising or other forms of revenue generation will be needed to keep brands solvent. In the end, a much more radical view of what makes a magazine will be required.

In 1613, the English cleric Samuel Purchas published *Purchas His Pilgrimage: or Relations of the World and the Religions observed in all Ages and Places discovered, from the Creation unto this Present*. In this ambitious work, which brought together travellers' accounts to explain the diversity of God's creation, he wrote of one church that under its porches were 'Magazines or Store-houses, wherein are kept lampes, oile, mats, and other necessaries'. It would not be for another century that the word magazine would be reduced to the dominant meaning that has lasted until today, a collection of written articles brought together in one publication.

In some respects, the magazines of the future may need to return to the older meaning of the word, as a storehouse for diverse things that are determined less by publishers themselves as by the readers who consume them. Apps such as Flipboard or Apple News do not virtually bind together digital versions of older print magazines but instead allow their users to select a huge range of sources and categories, creating personal magazines that they may even then publish to the wider world. In such an environment, editors are not the sole curators of those literary 'necessaries' that they commission and publish, but instead must join in with more active readers – and, indeed, software algorithms – to sort and collect together content that will entertain and inform.

Such a transition, should it happen, will not be a rapid one. There are still plenty of readers – and advertisers – as well as editors and publishers who have a preference for print. This shift would also bring its own challenges, not least of all financing and revenue (as any artist whose work is distributed via Spotify, for example, will tell you). Nonetheless, with the convergence of multiple media into single digital devices, more and more of us expect to do a variety of things, and read a variety of materials, on our smartphones and tablets. As such, the most successful magazines of the future are certain to look very different from the titles with which we are most familiar today.

Glossary

ABC: Audit Bureau of Circulations; with the BPA one of the main bodies that verifies how many copies of a title are distributed

advertorial: advertising feature designed to look like editorial; also known as an advertising feature

affinity sales: magazines sold in specialist shops that are sympathetic to the title; for example a music magazine in a music store

audit: an independent check by a body such as ABC or BPA to verify copies in circulation

average net circulation: the average number of copies produced per issue, which may be measured as paid net circulation (that is copies sold)

B2B: business-to-business; professional titles formerly known as trade magazines aimed at a specific industry

bar code: the machine readable strip of bars on a cover that contains information such as price and title

bimonthly/biweekly: a magazine published once every two months or two weeks

binding: means of fastening pages together, typically saddle-stitch (stapling) or perfect (glue)

bit map: an image described as a series of coloured pixels on screen

bleed: printing beyond the boundary of the page so that, once it is trimmed, ink goes right to the edge of the page

body copy: the main text of a page

BPA: Business Publications Audit, Inc.; along with ABC the main organisation that verifies magazine circulation

BRAD: British Rates and Data; monthly publication that lists newspaper and magazine titles in the UK

brief: the summary of what an article should consist of when commissioned by an editor

bulk sales: discounted copies that are sold in bulk to a company, such as a hotel or airline, that often gives them free to customers

bureau: an external company used to prepare films from digital files

byline: journalist's name given with an article

camera ready copy: a layout ready to be photographed to make plates

caption: text associated with a picture and providing additional information

centre spread: centre pages of a saddle-stitched magazine

churn: the rate of turnover in subscribers each year

classified advertising: advertising sold by the column or centimetre, as opposed to display advertising sold by the page

close: to finish production and send the magazine to the printers

CMYK: cyan, magenta, yellow and black, the four inks typically used in full-colour printing

colour proof: a high-quality representation of how a page will look once printed

colour separation: the four plates of CMYK ink used to create a full-colour print

commissioning: the process of hiring a freelance writer or artist to produce content for a magazine

consumer magazines: titles aimed at the general public, as opposed to B2B or specialist publications

contract publishing: publishing magazines for a third party

controlled circulation: distribution of a magazine free to specified individuals, for example those working in a particular industry

copyright: the legal ownership of creative work

cover mount: free gift attached to the front of a magazine

CPM: cost per mil (sometimes mille), or cost per thousand: the cost of reaching a thousand readers or advertisers with a page or publication

Cromalin: brand name for one type of colour proof

CTP: computer to plate; creating a plate using a laser to remove the need for film

defamation: a false statement that will harm the reputation of another person

demographic: information about a magazine audience, including such things as age, income and socio-economic status (ABC1/C2DE)

direct to plate: another way of referring to CTP

display advertising: advertising sold by the page rather than column centimetres

distributor: company responsible for getting a magazine from the printer to the consumer, whether via a store or via subscription

DPI: dots per inch; a way of measuring the resolution of scanners and printers

DPS: double-page spread; feature or advertising over two pages

drop cap: initial letter at the beginning of an article or paragraph that is larger than the surrounding text

DTP: desktop publishing; software used to lay out pages on computer

dummy: mock-up of a magazine produced to test how it will be received

ed/ad ratio: the ratio of editorial pages to advertising

editor: person in charge of a magazine or section of a magazine

editorial: material produced by journalists working for the magazine, but also articles expressing the opinion of the editor or publication

editorial assistant: someone who provides support for the editorial staff, such as answering phones and checking that invoices are submitted to the finance department

EPoS: electronic point of sale; information stored on computer whenever an item is sold

e-zine: electronic magazine, usually on the web

facing matter: advertising that faces appropriate editorial

fair comment: a defence against certain libel actions

fair use: the ability to copy a certain amount of material without permission from the copyright holder

film: a photographic representation of a page, usually on acetate, that is used to make printing plates

firm sale: titles paid for and not returnable

flat-plan: a map of a magazine issue that shows where editorial and advertising pages will appear

font: a set of characters, different sizes and styles

footer: information at the bottom of a page

format: the size and shape of a page, such as A4

gatefold: a page, usually inside the cover, that opens out to accommodate extra advertising

gone to bed: when a magazine is at the printers and cannot be modified

grid: the underlying structure of a page design that determines the position of such things as columns and pictures

gutter: the blank space between facing pages of a publication

hard copy: text on paper rather than screen

header: information at the top of a page

house ad: advertisement placed in a magazine by the publisher rather than external advertiser

house style: the set of rules that determines such things as spellings for disputed words, punctuation and use of numerals

HTML: hypertext markup language

ICC: International Colour Consortium; the body that governs standards for colour processing and printing

indent: text placed further away from the edge of the page than other copy, leaving white space

InDesign: standard page layout package used to produce magazines

insert: loose advertising or other material that is inserted between magazine pages

IPSO: Independent Press Standards Organisation; the UK press industry regulator that was established in September 2014 to replace the PCC

ISSN: International Standard Serial Number; a unique number assigned to every magazine

JPEG: file format used for digital images

justification: the alignment of text on one or both sides of a column or page

kerning: moving letters closer together so that they fit more neatly

kill fee: payment made for an article that is not used

layout: the design of a page, combining text and graphical elements

leading: the vertical space between lines of type

libel: a published statement that is defamatory

listings: brief details of events

literal: a spelling mistake

lithography: the underlying technology behind most printing; originally printing via stone (hence litho), but now usually metal and sometimes plastic plates

lower case: text that is not capitalised

LPI: lines per inch; the measure of resolution of film, as opposed to DPI

malicious falsehood: defamatory statement against products rather than individuals or organisations

masthead: the title of a magazine

matchprint: brand name of a colour proofing system

mechanical data: information about page sizes, bleed and trim sizes

media pack: information about a magazine's brand, its readers and advertising rates for potential advertisers

model-release form: agreement signed by a photographer's model, allowing the magazine to use the image

net paid circulation: total circulation for all copies of a magazine, where the consumer pays at least half the cover price

newsletter: publication with basic production values and distributed via subscription

NRS: National Readership Survey; organisation that conducts demographic research for publications in the UK

off the record: a statement made with restrictions as to how it can be reported or attributed

offset litho printing: the main technique of printing, where ink from a metal plate is transferred to a rubber sheet before being printed onto paper

on spec: material offered to an editor that has not been commissioned, on the chance that it might be used

on the record: a statement that may be publicly communicated

overheads: publishing costs not directly related to the business of magazine production

overrun: additional copies of an issue above the set print run

page rate: the cost for taking out a page of advertising in a magazine

page yield: revenues made from advertising sold on page

part work: a magazine designed to be collected over a series of issues

PCC: Press Complaints Commission; a self-regulatory body dealing with ethical issues in the UK press (closed in September 2014)

PDF: Portable Document Format; a file format for distributing files digitally and much used in printing

perfect binding: pages cut and glued together to form a spine

plate: the metal (sometimes plastic) sheet that carries an image of a page and is inked for printing

point of sale material: promotional materials used to attract consumers where a magazine is sold

post-mortem: the meeting after a magazine has been printed, to discuss what worked and what did not

Postscript: computer language describing elements of a page for printing

PPA: Professional Publishers Association; the main industry body representing magazines in the UK

pre-flight: process of checking a file for any potential errors before it is sent to the printer

print run: the total number of copies printed for an issue

proof: a copy of a page used to check that information is accurate before printing

PTC: Periodicals Training Council

publisher: the person responsible for the business side and profitability of a magazine

QuarkXPress: popular page-layout software

rate card: information showing how much it costs to advertise in a magazine and including other mechanical data

reach: the percentage of a target audience reading a magazine or advertisement

readership: people who read a magazine as opposed to those who actively buy it

registration: the correct alignment of the four plates used in colour printing

renewal rate: the number of readers who renew their subscription

repro: reproduction; the film and plate-making process of production

RIP: raster image processor; a machine that converts digital data into film as part of the repro process

saddle-stitch binding: originally sewn binding, but a magazine bound by stapling

spot colour: a single colour in addition to black

standfirst: introductory text following the title of an article

strapline: a heading just above or below another heading

style sheet: in DTP a series of formatting options that can be applied to such things as text and paragraphs

sub: a sub-editor, or shorthand for a subscription

supplement: a one-off magazine or magazine published as part of a newspaper

TIFF: image file format used for graphics

TMAP: Teen Magazine Arbitration Panel; a self-regulatory body dealing with teenage magazines

trim marks: crosses on the page showing the printer where the page should be cut after printing

typeface: complete set of characters in a particular design

web offset printing: a common form of printing where paper is fed from huge rolls, or webs

white space: use of white space around images or text to enhance design

Bibliography

Abrahamson, D. and Prior-Miller, M.R. (2015) *The Routledge Handbook of Magazine Research: The Future of the Magazine Form*, London and New York: Routledge.

Benwell, B. (2003) *Masculinity and Men's Lifestyle Magazines*, Oxford: Blackwell Publishing.

Bourdieu, P. (1986) 'The Forms of Capital', in J.G. Richardson (ed.), *The Handbook of Theory: Research for the Sociology of Education* (pp. 241–58), New York: Greenwood Press.

Butler, J., Holden, K. and Lidwell, W. (2007) *Universal Principles of Design*, Beverly, MA: Rockport Publishers.

Conboy, M. (2004) *Journalism: A Critical History*, London: Sage.

Consterdine, G. (2005) *How Magazine Advertising Works*, London: PPA Marketing.

Crowley, D. (2006) *Magazine Covers*, second edition, London: Mitchell Beazley.

Daly, C.P., Patrick, H. and Ryder, E. (1997) *The Magazine Publishing Industry*, Needham Heights, MA: Allyn & Bacon.

Dodd, M. and Hanna, M. (2015) *McNae's Essential Law for Journalists*, eighteenth edition, Oxford: Oxford University Press.

Durrani, A. (2015) 'The End of the Magazine Business as We Know it', *Campaign*, 4 June. http://www.campaignlive.co.uk/article/end-magazine-business-know/1349740 (accessed 20 January 2016).

Elam, K. (2004) *Grid Systems: Principles of Organizing Type*, New York: Princeton Architectural Press.

Fleishman, G. (2014) 'How Newsstand Failed the Magazine, and What Apple Should Do', *Macworld*, 30 October.

Fletcher, A. (2001) *The Art of Looking Sideways*, London: Phaidon.

Fletcher, K. (2005) *The Journalist's Handbook*, Basingstoke: Macmillan.

Franklin, B., Hamer, M., Hanna, M., Kinsey, M. and Richardson, J. (2005) *Key Concepts in Journalism*, London: Sage.

Frost, C. (2010) *Reporting for Journalists*, London: Routledge.

Frost, C. (2011) *Designing for Newspapers and Magazines*, London: Routledge.

Gauntlett, D. (2002) *Media, Gender and Identity: An Introduction*, London: Routledge.

Glaser, M. (2005) 'Future of Magazines: Net Could Empower Readers', www.ojr.org/ojr/stories/050524glaser (accessed 20 January 2016).

Glaser, M. (2009) 'Magazines Need to Embrace Multimedia Storytelling in Digital Age', *Mediashift*, mediashift.org/2009/08/magazines-need-to-embrace-multimedia-storytelling-in-digital-age239/ (accessed 20 January 2016).

Gough-Yates, A. (2002) *Understanding Women's Magazines*, London: Routledge.

Hamilton, N. (2007) *Magazine Writing*, London: Longman.

Harcup, T. (2015) *Journalism: Principles and Practice*, London: Sage.

Hennessy, B. (2005) *Writing Feature Articles*, fourth edition, St Louis, MO: Focal Press.

Hermes, J. (1995) *Reading Women's Magazines: An Analysis of Everyday Media Use*, London: Polity Press.

Hicks, W. (2002) *Subediting for Journalists*, London: Routledge.

Hicks, W. (2013) *English for Journalists*, London: Routledge.

Hicks, W. and Adams, S. (2009) *Interviewing for Journalists*, London: Routledge.

Hicks, W., Adams, S. and Gilbert, H. (2008) *Writing for Journalists*, London: Routledge.

Holderman, K.N. (2013) *Life After Print: Revising the Digital Editorial Strategy in Magazine Publishing*, publishing.sfu.ca.

Hutchison, E.R. (2007) *Art of Feature Writing: From Newspaper Features and Magazine Articles to Commentary*, Oxford: Oxford University Press.

Jackson, P. and Stevenson, N. (2001) *Making Sense of Men's Magazines*, London: Polity Press.

Johnson, S. and Prijatel, P. (1999) *Magazine Publishing*, London: McGraw-Hill.

Johnson, S. and Prijatel, P. (2006) *The Magazine from Cover to Cover*, second edition, Oxford: Oxford University Press.

King, S. (2001) *Magazine Designs that Work*, Beverly, MA: Rockport Publishers.

Lanson, J. and Stephens, M. (2007) *Writing and Reporting the News*, third edition, Oxford: Oxford University Press.

Leslie, J. (2003) *Magculture: New Magazine Design*, London: Laurence King Publishing.

Lupton, E. (2004) *Thinking with Type: A Critical Guide for Designers, Writers, Editors, and Students*, New York: Princeton Architectural Press.

McCracken, E. (1992) *Decoding Women's Magazines: From 'Mademoiselle' to 'Ms'*, Basingstoke: Palgrave Macmillan.

McKane, A. (2004) *Journalism: A Career Handbook*, London: A & C Black.

McKay, J. (2013) *The Magazines Handbook*, London: Routledge.

McLoughlin, L. (2000) *The Language of Magazines*, London: Routledge.

McNair, B. (2009) *News and Journalism in the UK*, London: Routledge.

Madrigal, A. (2012) 'Dark Social: We Have the Whole History of the Web Wrong', *The Atlantic*, 12 October. www.theatlantic.com/technology/archive/2012/10/dark-social-we-have-the-whole-history-of-the-web-wrong/263523/ (accessed 13 June 2016).

Marr, A. (2005) *My Trade: A Short History of British Journalism*, London: Pan.

Marsh, P. (2014) 'The State of Paid Content: For Free, for a Fee, or Somewhere in Between', www.inma.org/blogs/ahead-of-the-curve/post.cfm/the-state-of-paid-content-for-free-for-a-fee-or-somewhere-in-between (accessed 20 January 2016).

Mason, P. and Smith, D. (1998) *Magazine Law: A Practical Guide*, London: Routledge.

Morgan, P. (2005) *The Insider: The Private Diaries of a Scandalous Decade*, London: Ebury Press.

Morrish, J. (2003) *Magazine Editing: How to Develop and Manage a Successful Publication*, London: Routledge.

Morrish, J. and Bradshaw, P. (2013) *Magazine Editing: In Print and Online*, London: Routledge.

Pelusy, M. and Pelusy, J. (2005) *The Media: Magazines*, New York: Chelsea House Publishers.

Petulla, S. (2014) 'Why You Need to Stop Using the Term "Brand Journalism"', *Contently*, 13 October. https://contently.com/strategist/2014/10/13/why-you-need-to-stop-using-the-term-brand-journalism/ (accessed 20 January 2016).

Phillips, A. (2007) *Good Writing for Journalists*, London: Sage.

Randall, D. (2007) *The Universal Journalist*, London: Pluto Press.

Renard, D. (2006) *The Last Magazine: Magazines in Transition*, New York: Universe Publishing.

Rivers, C. (2006) *Mag-art: Innovation in Magazine Design and Packaging*, Hove: Rotovision.

Rocha, T. (2000) *Magazine Publishing*, New York: Rosen Publishing.

Samara, T. (2005) *Making and Breaking the Grid: A Layout Design Workshop*, Beverly, MA: Rockport Publishers.

Stamm, D. and Scott, A. (2014) *Inside Magazine Publishing*, London: Routledge.

Strunk, W. (2013) *The Elements of Style*, London: Longman.

Taylor, S. and Brody, N. (2006) *100 Years of Magazine Covers*, London: Black Dog Publishing.

Theberge, P. (1997) *Any Sound You Can Imagine: Making Music/Consuming Technology*, Middletown, CT: Wesleyan University Press.

White, J.V. (2003) *Editing by Design: For Designers, Art Directors and Editors, the Classic Guide to Winning Readers*, third edition, New York: Allworth Press.

Yopp, J.J. and McAdams, K.C. (2006) *Reaching Audiences: A Guide to Media Writing*, Needham Heights, MA: Allyn & Bacon.

Index